Poems for Her Majesty - In Celebration Of The Queen's 80th Birthday

Edited by Holly Crowson

First published in Great Britain in 2006 by:
Anchor Books
Remus House
Coltsfoot Drive
Peterborough
PE2 9JX
Telephone: 01733 898102
Website: www.forwardpress.co.uk

All Rights Reserved

© *Copyright Contributors 2006*

SB ISBN 1 84418 431 5

Foreword

Anchor Books is a small press, established in 1992, with the aim of promoting readable poetry to as wide an audience as possible.

We hope to establish an outlet for writers of poetry who may have struggled to see their work in print.

The poems presented here have been selected from many entries, and as always editing proved to be a difficult task.

I trust this selection will delight and please the authors and all those who enjoy reading poetry.

Holly Crowson

Editor

Contents

The Queen, Our Rose	Muhammad Khurram Salim	1
Memories Of A Royal Event	Linda Knight	1
80 Glorious Years (Elizabeth II HRH)	Jasmine King	2
Our Queen Elizabeth . . . Happy 80th Birthday	Angie Claxton	2
Her Radiant Majesty	Umar Azam	3
Thank You, Ma'am	Di Bagshawe	4
To The Queen	Joy Stillwell	5
Across The Green And Pleasant Land	Andrew Blakemore	6
In Honour Of Queen Elizabeth	Niloufer Khan	7
Happy Birthday, Ma'am	Julie Brown	8
Happy 80th Birthday, Your Majesty	Maria Sheikh	9
Our Wonderful Queen	Martin Selwood	10
Two Queens	John Tiong Chunghoo	11
See The Queen	Barry Ryan	12
Glory To The Queen	Seshu Chamarty	12
Long To Reign Over Us	Rose-Mary Gower	13
Her Royal Highness Birthday Greetings	Joan Prentice	13
The Queen's Reign	David Cameron	14
Cheers	W Curran	14
A Great Celebration	L A G Butler	15
Down Under - The Royal Couple's First Train Tour	June Hall	15
Your Majesty	Yvonne Watkin-Rees	16
Queen On Horseback	Patricia Anne Ray	16
Elizabeth R At Eighty	Kathy Johnson	17
Poem For The Queen	Kiri Deaves (11)	17
The Royal Second Mile	Martin Winbolt-Lewis	18
God Save The Queen	B W Ballard	19
Queen Elizabeth II	S Kinsey	20
Elizabeth Regina	Maureen Boyd Joines Anderson	20
Sonnet On The Queen's Birthday	Alan C Brown	21
The Queen	Barbara Brown	21
Lilibet At 80	Geoff Donkin	22

Gracious Queen	Royston E Herbert	23
Elizabeth, Crowned Queen In 1953	Joyce Hemsley	24
Happy Birthday, Your Majesty!	Matthew Pickhaver	25
Happy Birthday	Daphne Cornell	26
The Queen	Pat Wearn	26
For You	Samantha Douglas	27
Lady Of Britain	R Pang	27
Birthday Greetings	Steve Glason	28
In Praise Of Our Queen	Pamela Carder	29
Royal Visit In The Rain	Doreen M Bowers	30
A Contemporary Salutes Her Majesty . . .	Jim Morgan	31
The Queen	Gordon Andrews	32
Poem To The Queen	Sylvia Dyer	32
Happy Birthday, Your Majesty	Samuel McAlister	33
The Queen's 80th Birthday	D McDonald	33
Eighty Glorious Years	Georgina Johnston	34
April 21, 2006	Margaret Ann Wheatley	35
God Bless The Queen At Eighty	Adrian Brett	36
She Rules With Grace	Ken Lou	36
Jubilant Heart Of Oak	John Worthington	37
I'd Love To Meet The Queen	Jay Berkowitz	37
Let Us Show	Ashok Chakravarthy	38
Elizabethan Ages	Roma Davies	39
HRH Queen Elizabeth II - Eighty Years Young	Jean Bald	40
Her Royal Highness The Queen At Eighty	Gina A Miller	40
Queen Elizabeth II	Christine Hardemon	41
Untitled	Barbara Collar	41
Year Of The Disabled	Richard Trowbridge	42
Our Sovereign Queen	Peter G Hoar	43
80th Birthday Wish For Queen Elizabeth	Elizabeth Anne Gifford	44
Birthday Bonus	A R Harcus	45
Our Queen	C M Pountney	46
Untitled	K M Abbott	46
Happy Birthday, Ma'am	Anne Marie Latham	47
To A Royal Octogenarian	Desmond Quick	48
Felicitations	R D Hiscoke	48

Birthday Congratulations	Jackie Richardson	49
Untitled	Lorraine Fisher	49
A Sovereign Lady	Marlene Allen	50
The Crown Of Royal Duty	M J Harris	50
A Job For Life	Valerie Hall	51
A Tribute To Her Majesty	Elizabeth Monk	51
Elizabeth II	Thora Carpenter	52
Sent From A Distance	Felix Oriseikwe Sylvanus	52
A Royal Pageant	Denise Castellani	53
Her Royal Smile	Cheryl Campbell	54
Meeting Of The Minds	Win Tipson	55
A Poem For Her Majesty	Beverley R Stepney	56
Our Queen	Maggie Strong	57
Poem For The Queen	Sarah Scott	57
Our Queen	Carol Bernadette Boneham	58
Queen Elizabeth	Jean Martin-Doyle	59
Our Queen Elizabeth II	Doris E Pullen	60
Greetings - Elizabeth II	Pauline Boncey	60
Queen Elizabeth's Birthday	Kathleen M Scatchard	61
A Poem To My Queen On Her Birthday! (Yay!)	Mathilda Lucas-Box (12)	61
Long May She Reign	Jean M Ellis	62
The Queen's 80th Birthday	Olivia Sumrie	62
The Queen	Sophie Greig (12)	63
The Queen's 80th Birthday Poem	Hannah-Louise Callaghan (12)	63
The River And The Ocean	T Anish	64
Elizabeth	Mavis Gould	64
Birthday Blessing!	Mary Skelton	65
Happy Birthday Ma'am	Shirley Pinnington	65
Blest Art Thee	Ann Crampton	66
The First Photograph	Michael Hartshorne	67
A Woman Behind The Crown	R S Wayne Hughes	68
May God Bless The Queen	Gary Jones	68
The Queen	Camille McCrosson (11)	69
The Queen's 80th Birthday Poem	Dorothy Robertson (12)	69
Happy Birthday Ma'am	Anton Nicholas	70
Eighty Years	Anne Everest	71
The Queen's 80th Birthday	Charlotte Emily Tucker (12)	72
The Queen's Poem	Lara Cameron (11)	72
Queen Elizabeth II	Grace Hollingsworth	73

The Queen's 80th Birthday	Philippa Batey (12)	73
Defender Of The Faith	Kathy Rawstron	74
Service To The Royal Family	Gordon E Miles	75
Your Majesty	Janet Scrivens	76
The Queen 2006	Edward Hill	76
Born Ter Be Queen	Jacqueline Claire Davies	77
Happy Birthday	Emily Culpeper (11)	77
The Heart Of Being Her Majesty	Glenwyn Peter Evans	78
To Your Majesty Queen Elizabeth	Jean McGovern	79
To The Queen	Daniella Humble (11)	80
The Queen	Katherine Mundy (11)	80
Her Majesty!	Kevin Clark	81
A Poem For The Queen	Matthew Willbye	81
The Nation's Mother	C M Armstrong	82
Hail The Queen	Ojuola Tolulope	82
Hail The Queen	Evelyn Oti	83
A Birthday Wish	Madeline Reade	83
My Inspiration	June Davies	84
In True Celebration	Dawn Prestwich	84
Happy Birthday, Ma'am	Ann Sutcliffe	85
Old Age Speckles	Hsu Chi Cheng	85
A Poem For The Queen	Alan Millard	86
Majesty	Rosemary Peach	87
The Corgi Story	Sarah Louise Parry	88
A Birthday Greeting For Her Majesty The Queen	Peter Spurgin	88
God Bless Her Majesty	Janet Cavill	89
Easter Royal	Evelyn M Harding	89
Our Queen	E B Soltys	90
The Queen - Your 80th Birthday	John Freeth	91
A Real Princess	Maureen Connolly (nee Creissen)	92
Coral Waves	Roger Mosedale	92
A Letter To Her Majesty Upon Her 80th Birthday	Jonel Abellanosa	93
The Queen - Her Way	Freda Grieve	94
Dear Ma'am	John L Wright	95
Queen Elizabeth II 80th Birthday	Olive Young	96

A Special Birthday	Maureen Steele	96
A Royal Celebration	Peter G H Payne	97
The Power And The Blood	Philip Loudon	97
Celebration	M S Bradley	98
Eightieth Birthday	Joy Saunders	98
Untitled	Wendy Deaves	99
To Our Queen - A Happy Birthday	Kathleen M Hatton	99
Here's To Elizabeth	Anne Wild	100
The Queen Of England	Anthony Rosato	101
Gratitude	James Melrose	102
Queen's 80th Birthday	Martha Ann D'Souza	103
The Queen	Aijaz Gul	104
The Queen Of Hearts	Tri Tran	104
Happy Easter And Happy Birthday Greetings	Valerie Ovais	105
Elizabeth Regina	Iris Ina Glatz	105
To Be A Head Of A Nation	Yoko Hand	106
Birthday Greetings To Elizabeth R	Jean Dutfield	106
Regal Respect	J W Whiteacre	107
Happy Birthday, Your Majesty	Malcolm G Bradshaw	108
Our Modern Monarch	Doreen E Hampshire	109
Easter Birthday	Patricia Arnett	110
Our Queen	M Wilcox	110
A Tribute	David Anderson	111
Her Majesty's Birthday	Ellen Spiring	112
Queen Elizabeth's 80th Birthday	Janet Wright	112
Tribute To Her Majesty	Bell Ferris	113
The Queen	Jeanette Gaffney	114
The Queen Is Eighty	Colin Metcalfe	114
One And All	Melody	115
Here's A Health Unto Your Majesty	Beryl Mapperley	115
Her Majesty The Queen - April 2006	Gwilym Beechey	116
Our Steadfast Rock	B Williams	116
The Queen's 80th Birthday	Finnan Boyle	117
A Toast	S Mullinger	117
An Easter Message - A Birthday Wish	Frances Gibson	118

Faeries And Queens	Gillian Muir	119
Easter 365	Laurence D E Calvert	120
Your Royal Majesty	Margaret Doherty	120
Regal Steps	Hale Tsehlana	121
A Poem For Her Majesty	Melissa Tindall (9)	121
The Birthday Girl - April 2006	Violet M Corlett	122
How Shall I Call You?	Margaret Rose Harris	123
Eighty Today	Annette Smith	124
Our Wonderful Queen	Joy Hall	124
The Queen's 80th Birthday	Graham Watkins	125
Paean	John Coombes	126
A Birthday Gift To The Queen	Raymond A Uyok	127
Quintessentially . . .	Helen Smith	128
Your Majesty	Averil Fairey	128
My Royal Nightmare	Thomas Dickinson	129
80th Birthday, Cake Of Memories	Angela Pritchard	129
The Queen	Jean Paisley	130
Queen Elizabeth II - 80th Birthday Verses	Patricia Mary Saunders	130
Blessings On D-Day	Ladee Basset	131
Elizabeth Our Queen	Peggy Howe	132
With Thanks To The Queen	Kerrie Washington	133
The Queen's 80th Birthday	Wila Yagel	134
Queen's 80th	M Shaw	134
EIIR - At 80 2006	N D Wood	135
A Poem For The Queen	Joyce Strong	135
Long Live The Queen!	Mark Walker	137
Happy Birthday, Ma'am	Rachel E Joyce	137
For Her Majesty's 80th Birthday	Meg Atkins	138
Glorious Majesty	Gillian Jones	138
Hail The Queen	Efua Sam-Avor	139
A Poem For Her Majesty	Rachael Milsted	139
Great Britain	Sheila Cheesman	140
Happy And Glorious	John V Waby	140
The Queen	Francis Arthur Rawlinson	141
Your Majesty	Valerie Sutton	141
Our Gracious Queen	A Audrey Agnew	142
God Bless You Ma'am	Alan Pow	143
Let All The Nation Sing	Peter Morriss	144
Lost Moment	Rosemary Cresswell	145

A Shared Experience	Stella Bush-Payne	146
Conqueror Of Hearts	Davis Akkara	147
God Bless The Queen	Oludotun Fajorin	148
Happy Birthday Your Highness	Ferrell L 'Huck' Hickson	149
My Memories From 1956 To 2006	Anjum Wasim Dar	150
The Queen (Public And Private)	Georgina Percivall	151
Happy Birthday	Louise Smith	152
Happy Birthday	Patricia Turpin	153
The Queen's 80th Birthday	Sandra Bentley	154
Your Majesty!	Edgar E Poole	155
A Tribute To Her Majesty	Peter R Beadle	156
Our Queen	Natalie Opray	157
The Crown	Jasmina Trifunovic	158
Our Majesty The Queen	Rosalind Sim	159
Congratulations	Dorothy Neil	160
Oh Great Queen	Adegoke Austin Adedamola	161
Children Of The Empire	Liz Davies	162
A Royal In The Ribble	Joyce Graham	163
For The Queen	Mary Guckian	164
The Queen And I	Bill Campbell	165
God Bless Our Queen	Valma June Streatfield	166

The Poems

The Queen, Our Rose

She is the symbol of our resolve
To not think paltry thoughts.
She is the harbinger,
The Queen, not just of the land
But of our hearts.
She is the rose, forever the rose.
Planted to last for such a long time.
Her twilight years have her
Playing among the blossoms.
She has a heart of gold.
We'll aim high, we'll try to
Rid the world of greed.
Indeed she helps us to know
How to make the big show.
Elizabeth Monarch, paves the way
For a fluorescent new day.

Muhammad Khurram Salim

Memories Of A Royal Event

All the family gathered round at Grandad's house to see
the coronation of our Queen, filmed by the BBC.
I thought it was amazing to see a real life queen
appearing like a film star on our black and white small screen.
The Queen looked very pretty, wearing sparkling jewels and crown,
and dress so very beautiful, with long cloak hanging down.
She sat inside the golden coach and smiled, on this, her day,
and eight white horses pulled the coach along the crowded way.

I can remember Father taking me along our street,
and riding on his shoulders, I kicked out my little feet.
I was only nearly five with freckles and red hair
and it was pouring down with rain, I didn't really care.
All the neighbours gathered round to party and have fun
to celebrate this special day in June for everyone.

Linda Knight

80 Glorious Years (Elizabeth II HRH)

First a princess, then 'Queen of a nation'
We celebrate one, deserving of our adoration.
Brows circled with ancient jewelled crown - of state,
Wears her duties, many mantled gown - proud, sedate.

Light of our nation; crowds gather where she is seen,
To cheer and wave, to the loving hand of a joyful Queen.
They stand for hours, to gaze beyond pomp - and ceremony,
And see a dedicated woman, a mother, head of a royal family.

Sad when misrepresented or misunderstood,
Remains, through bad times and through good.
Whose grace, and smiling countenance - never fails,
Finds solace in her horses, and corgis' stumpy, wagging tails.

A second sun, she shines as brightly as the first
God grant Her Majesty many more, happy not worst.
We wish you a day of celebrations and fun - and tradition,
In the merry month of April; in this great realm - this England.

Jasmine King

Our Queen Elizabeth . . . Happy 80th Birthday

Our Queen Elizabeth, our monarch,
you reign with so much grace,
admired and respected by all
of the human race.

So today, upon your 80th birthday, Ma'am,
I send you all my best wishes,
that you have a most perfect day,
and enjoy your celebrations.

Angie Claxton

Her Radiant Majesty

With a dazzling smile which is sure to please,
She reins over the country with the greatest of ease!
Still competent as ever at eighty years of age,
Greater love for our monarch is hard to envisage!

Appointed by God most high to serve the nation,
Her affectionate nature fills us all with admiration!
Having her as Queen has become Britain's wont;
A republic we would hate, not something we want!

She lives in a palace and rides a golden coach;
But her manner is humble and she is easy to approach!
Owner of riches and many a gem;
Her Maj is the gem, forget about them!

Stunning she looks, whatever her attire;
Opening Parliament, or by the palace fire!
Lucky is the Duke to have her as wife;
Enduring marital bliss, absence of strife!

On the Queen's train or flying abroad;
Her Majesty's travels are formidably broad!
Shaking the hands of Presidents and Heads of State;
She fulfils monarchal duties, date after date!

Her crystal voice does utter words with care;
Never does she shun the camera's glare!
Her crown does sparkle, with many a ray;
May this throne accommodate her, day after day!

A duty of hers is to compile honours' lists,
To let the nation learn the names of its firsts!
Such a list of names has there frequently been,
But who will *honour* Her Majesty The Queen?

Umar Azam

Thank You, Ma'am

Your Majesty,
As one of your generation, Ma'am,
May I acknowledge the debt
Of example I owe to you,
Your childhood too influenced mine.
Even informal portraits show you smiling
Or quietly serene.
That smile has done so much
To encourage and show gratitude
And a very real sense of humour.
Always elegant when 'on duty',
Yet happily relaxed in your loved countryside.
Unfailingly gracious, the correct touch,
To all of any status or nationality;
Never visibly bored with repetitive engagements
Despite long hours and travelling.
Ma'am, you are as we all would be,
As monarch, mother, and grandmother,
Loved equally by those you meet,
And those who stand in the crowd.
The link between past and present,
Surpassing your subjects in devoted duty -
In present knowledge and comprehension of events;
Holding in your hand and head
More than half a century of experience.
Your faith and principles are a light
In time's bewildering changes.
A loyal toast to Your Majesty,
Your accession was the best gift
Our country and commonwealth
Could have been privileged to receive,
Long may we enjoy it.

Di Bagshawe

To The Queen
(In honour of your 80th birthday)

Your Majesty, you do wear well
Just like your mother before you!
You have strength of character
Given from our Lord;
As you trust Him each day
He keeps you in the right way.

Your early years were full of love
With father, mother and sister;
Also the little corgis,
Who played near to you
And the horses you rode well,
Which helped you later in parades.

Then came wartime, sad for all
With lives lost, here and abroad.
As a family, each of you
Showed your sympathy,
By joining the Forces, caring
For wounded, helping where you could.

But a happy occasion came
When you got engaged to Philip.
A handsome prince, and royal bride
Drove in carriage of gold,
To Westminster Abbey to wed,
Then on honeymoon at Balmoral.

Next came the news of your son's birth,
The first of your four dear children.
When visiting Kenya, your father died,
In faith you became our Queen.
You're a shining example to us all
So enjoy your 80th birthday.

Joy Stillwell

Across The Green And Pleasant Land

Across the green and pleasant land,
Nurtured by your caring hand,
As if a rock you firmly stand,
While winds of change do blow.
Across the seas that reach so wide,
To distant countries to abide,
To calm the waves and ocean tide,
So gently they will flow.

Across the mountains, fields and hill,
The towns and cities joy instil,
Forever reign, it is God's will,
Long may it always be.
Across the nations great and small,
Love shall truly conquer all,
Your flag of honour shall not fall,
And always fly so free.

Across the blue and endless sky,
And through the storms of tumult fly,
So peace will reign and never die,
Our time shall not forget.
Across horizons dawn each day,
Your true light will guide our way,
And all our hopes and dreams will stay,
Until the sun does set.

Andrew Blakemore

In Honour Of Queen Elizabeth

Destined to be the one and only unique personality.
Never tired or dismayed.
Cutting short her honeymoon to reign and fulfil her onerous duties.
Head of the Commonwealth, extending help to members the
world over.
Having a fairy-tale coach wedding with love and support from
her husband, family and subjects.
Bearing domestic disasters of daughters-in-law with quiet reserve
and calmness.
Visiting daily charitable institutions with a smile here and a shake of
the hand there.
Symbolising and emanating power, prestige and warmth of
personality.
A lover of horses and corgis has made her a world authority on horses
and horse racing.
Gone through traumatic experiences of losing her sister and mother
and the dramatic tragedy of Lady Diana.
Emotions she bore with equanimity to allow her son to marry again.
What a stupendous personality.
She is no other than Her Majesty Elizabeth Queen of England.
We all salute her on her 80th birthday.
Widely travelled, may she rule longer with love from the family and
admiration from the world, like a lighthouse emanating light to guard
and guide ships on rough waters.
She is everybody's Queen!

Niloufer Khan

Happy Birthday, Ma'am

A very happy birthday
to Elizabeth our Queen.
Down through the years
what changes she has seen.

She met a handsome sailor
and married him in style.
We were all so happy
as she walked down the aisle.

Then came her coronation
another time for joy,
and by this time
they had a girl and boy.

She rules her beloved country
with all the love and care.
In times of great crisis
she is always there.

Through wars she's brought us
and taught us how to smile.
Through the very worst times
she went that extra mile.

Now she's reached that milestone
and after eighty years,
good health to your Majesty
God bless, and many cheers.

Julie Brown

Happy 80th Birthday, Your Majesty

Happy 80th birthday to Your Majesty
May God bless you always wherever you will be
You are one of the wonders of the world
From Heaven above you were gently hurled
The sweet angels came down to you one by one
When you were born the angels still looked on
Your eyes light your crown in full glory and strength
Your country you protect at any length
Your own personal problems you just put to one side
With your head held high as you walk with poise and pride
Your laughter and smile just tells it all
You have everyone at your devoted beckoning call
Your beauty embarrasses the sweet beautiful red rose
Your love, care and gentle nature grows and grows
Your love for animals shows all your beauty from within
Your corgis are charming, cute, healthy and trim
Your people love you more than you can ever know
Our heads are bowed down in respect because we love you so
Your strength, your power, grows with each hour
Your head is held high and mighty in every type of situation
Your treasured name and love is spread throughout every country
                                                         and nation
Wishing you a long life, good health, good wealth and prosperity
Good luck for the future and hope it's potentially stress free
Your Majesty, your people from their hearts and souls wish to
                                                       honourably say
Wishing you a fantastic memorable happy 80th birthday.

Maria Sheikh

Our Wonderful Queen

Our Queen - so serene
So stately - one of the best
Standing head and shoulders
Way above the rest

Since her coronation day
When she made that 'declaration'
She has remained firm
In every situation

When difficulties became apparent
Our Queen has stood steadfast
Overcoming her several problems
With a strength we know will last

Dearly loved by all her subjects
In our country - far and wide
Remaining strong and loyal
Whatever may betide

Now nearing eighty
Her resolve ever stronger
May she retain her position
Her reign becoming longer

So - raise your glasses
Shout, 'Hip hip hooray!'
For it's our monarch's birthday
So let's have a glorious day.

Martin Selwood

Two Queens

An historic queen used to flip through
my little hands - little square,
round coppers, round nickels, blue and green notes
one cent, five, ten cents, one dollar, five dollars
which could buy so much more.
The alluring queen with a dazzling smile
tinkled in Dad's foot-deep pockets,
Mom's and Aunty's humble PVC handbags,
and late Granny's secret pocket
in her blouse as we little tots
pestered them for money for things
we longed for day and night.
There was brother's unforgettable
red Raleigh, the wooden wall clock
with a flying horse that had seen better days,
Christmas vinyl records, poetry books.
They were all acquired with smiles -
ours and the Queen's we still hold dear to our hearts.
The Queen still tinkles, tinkles
in our mind despite all these rolling years.
So many things spill over
from the British to independent years.
Topping them could be found in Mom's crown
- she so loves the Queen's simple, clean
curly silky crop, she ingeniously
copies her style to this day.
The Queen, the British Queen,
she is such a beauty, she would say
every time she came on television.
And every time I see the Queen, I actually
see two queens and will always.

John Tiong Chunghoo

See The Queen

One day, I would love to take Hannah to London (as she is very keen),
even look at the gates of H M The Queen!
Tell her, that Her Majesty is 80 years old,
plus other information that should be told!

The Queen was born at 17 Brunswick Square
and has four royal heirs,
HRH Charles, Anne, Andy and Edward,
also have staff, over several hundred!

Been on the throne for 53 years,
(love it when people cheer)!
Queen Victoria had 64 years' reign,
(So, Ma'am, you have another 20 years to maintain)!

Surrounded by Prince Philip and her corgi dogs,
walking early at Windsor Castle, in the fog!
Ten Prime Ministers the Queen's had,
some were good, the others were bad!
People sing 'God Save our Gracious Queen'
from towns and cities to village greens.

Barry Ryan

Glory To The Queen

Glory to Her Majesty be
as world regal personified
in her grace and warmth,
the hoary past in goodwill
a royal family could bring,
epitomised in her character!

Let the Lord shower
His blessings truly
on her glowing smile,
and evidence the hope
for greater peace and amity
that shall rule the Earth
like before and forever.

Seshu Chamarty

Long To Reign Over Us

Accepting the weight of untimely majesty,
Although young, you shouldered your obligation,
Assuming an austere and regal countenance,
You commanded the respect of the nation,
The intervening years have marched on relentlessly,
The old century slipped into the twenty-first,
And still you dutifully serve your people
Through the good times and some of the worst,
Faced with criticism, heartbreak and sorrow,
You are forbearing, steadfast and brave,
You will not relinquish your wearisome burden
Vowing to see your assignment through to the grave,
At eighty you are undiminished in courage and grace,
All God's richest blessings be upon you, Your Majesty
And give you endurance for what you still have to face.

Rose-Mary Gower

Her Royal Highness Birthday Greetings

A long time ago when our Queen was born
An Easter-time baby, when I was just four
As I grew older and learned of our Queen
I delighted in stories about places she'd been.

This princess, her progress I followed through life
So delightful with elegance, even through strife
I knew one day she would rule over this land
As always with royalty, her future was planned.

King George and Queen Mother, her mum and dad
The loveliest of parents, the best you could have
Elizabeth was groomed for her future ahead
With courtesy, patience, and tolerance it's said.

Eight decades, our Queen has blossomed and grown
In wars and bereavements, her smile is well known
Her smiles are the same as when I was young
Now her eightieth birthday, all hearts she has won.

Joan Prentice

The Queen's Reign

Surrounded by controversy from the present and the past
The Queen has reigned magnificent through this century and the last
Leading by example she has led the country through good and bad
And to hear the anti-royalists diminish her reign, really is quite sad
Taking all the criticism and never once being allowed to have her say
Expresses the commitment that she made on coronation day
And how she has held together the countries far and wide
From modern day success stories, to disasters we cannot hide
The gathering of the Commonwealth to defend a common cause
Bringing together poorer nations, I think she deserves applause
But I do have reservations about her children's commitment to reign
Their divorces have left the monarchy with much heartache and pain
When the pressures were too great to sort their problems out
They wilted and conceded failure instead of turning it about
So what about the future on the Queen's eightieth birthday?
Has she made her mind up? Will she go or will she stay?
What can replace her presence when she decides to go?
In this world of real uncertainty, her absence is bound to show
But like any other pensioner, the time must surely dawn
For her to retire gracefully and awake to a brand new dawn
And then, like the rest of us, when her time has finally come
To head out to the great unknown, to that empire beyond the sun.

David Cameron

Cheers

As Queen there's no way you can retire,
No slippers and book beside a log fire,
You continue to serve your country so well,
Down through the years we are under your spell,
As your family surrounds you,
In your eightieth year,
Happy birthday, Ma'am,
From your subjects - cheers!

W Curran

A Great Celebration

All your life a royal lady you have been
But you were not born to be our Queen
Fate stepped in and placed you on the throne
You married Philip your prince, so you were not alone
Your marriage was blessed with a daughter and three sons
Each birth your subjects rejoiced and blessed each one
You have reigned over us for a very long time
Through times of darkness you made things shine
You have presided over events both great and small
To the credit of Britain and in the eyes of us all
Like all parents your family gave you some tears
They have now settled down in their mature years
You have worked far into your pensionable age
The throne is a rock with you at its head, we are made
To meet you in person is most people's dream
We toast you today and wish a happy birthday
To you our *Queen*.

L A G Butler

Down Under - The Royal Couple's First Train Tour

Strap-hanging, in love,
they spy a flag of live sheep
dyed blue, white and red.

White-gloved, the young queen waves, her
smile rippling round the Empire.

June Hall

Your Majesty

Over eight decades you have lived your life
As a loving daughter and then a wife,
A famous mother of children four,
A grandmother proud of even more.
The inspiring monarch of the British Nation
You have served our country with dedication,
And then, when travelling far and wide,
With Prince Philip at your side,
You've engendered heartfelt commendation,
And from young and old their admiration.

As Head of State, since you were enthroned,
A 'private' life you have hardly owned,
For daily duties of generous measure
Have much curtailed your hours of leisure.
But with dignity and gentle grace
You've put a smile on many a face,
And when quite soon, on a special date,
Your Eightieth ear you will celebrate,
We trust and hope and sincerely pray
It will be for you such a happy day!
May God bless you, Ma'am!

Yvonne Watkin-Rees

Queen On Horseback

Down in the woods
All is calm and green,
Here comes the Queen
With a smile so serene,
As she rides her tall horse
For mile upon mile,
Looking very high
Under the blue sky.

Patricia Anne Ray

Elizabeth R At Eighty

When Elizabeth Alexandra Mary was born - jubilation,
Became a monarch through - abdication
Her father was King - his coronation
Then came his sad funeral - oration.

Elizabeth pledged her life to the - nation
She became wife to Philip - much elation
Motherhood mixed with - ceremonial occasion
Horses and dogs are her - relaxation

Ambassadors present her with - accreditation
Representing every far-flung - nation
She has travelled this world in plush - accommodation
Bringing a smile in greeting - felicitation

Family life has had some - vexation
Newspapers filled with the latest royal - sensation
Elizabeth has risen above this, no - recrimination
From the monarch who knows her - royal station

Well has she served this land going through - modernisation
She has enhanced the - royal constitution
Let us all say happy birthday in the normal - tradition
And all her subjects join Her Majesty in - celebration.

Kathy Johnson

Poem For The Queen

For so many years now you have been the Queen
what great things have come and been?
Sad and happy things but you got through
so happy birthday from me to you.

Kiri Deaves (11)

The Royal Second Mile

Around the globe in eighty years
The birthday Queen, she knows no fear;
Like facing down the grisly Haka;
This lady monarch's quite a cracker!

From royal yacht to sonic jet
She heads the moving, shaking set;
The countries feted, nationals met . . .
Her Majesty is partying yet!

Elizabeth the Second moves
On wheels, on keels, on foot and hooves -
Her liveried cohorts chasing hard
To give Queen Liz a royal guard.

She strolls around Buck House's grounds
Remembering names before the rounds
Of garden parties, and openings,
And other dreary kinds of things.

She glides in pinks and blues and yellow,
In dresses bright, pastel and mellow,
To make the dullest walkabout
A thing for folk to talk about!

The royal corgis share her passion
For ditching her official fashion,
By chewing up those ghastly hats
As bedding for the Windsor cats!

Resplendent in her limes and creams
. . . *'One's realised so many dreams'* . . .
Like eating roast bat in the tropics
Whilst savouring all the hottest topics.

This year of celebration beckons
As many a royal pundit reckons,
Future years of much endeavour;
With *'Abdicate? Me? Never!'*

Martin Winbolt-Lewis

God Save The Queen

The majority of subjects all love their Queen
We think she's the greatest there's ever been
She loves her country, playing a dutiful role
Into which she places her heart and soul.

Placed on the throne at such a young age
So many memories, turning each scrapbook page
She is totally immersed in the sport of kings
And revels in the excitement which it brings.

She always attends the last night of the proms
She visits that land where they call us 'Poms'
Ladies-in-waiting will be called to her side
A golden coach in which sometimes she will ride.

She has led such an extraordinary life
As a mother, grandmother, sovereign and wife
Known for a love of breeding racehorses
Which she loves to see run at various courses.

She an ambassador of the finest kind
People she meets say she's polite and refined
She befits her role as our Head of State
The roles she performs, she is simply first rate.

A visit from the Prime Minister every week
An update on political situations, she will seek
There is one thing which brings no acclaim
When grouse season arrives, they shoot for game.

Flags will start waving when she appears
The crowds are enthralled, yelling their cheers
In a limousine she sits, giving a wave of the hand
She was born into this life, that we must understand.

On the palace roof was to be seen
Brian May, playing 'God Save The Queen'
Speeches easily roll off her tongue,
Loved by all, the elderly and the young.

B W Ballard

Queen Elizabeth II
(1952 - 2006)

Queen Elizabeth has reigned for fifty-four years,
She's had her fair share of heartaches, and shed a few tears,
But she has come through the sorrow, that she's had to bear,
With the nation behind her, showing how much they care.
On her 80th birthday, on her walkabout in the town,
Her number one fan gave her a cake in the shape of her crown.
Hope she enjoyed it and had a slice with her afternoon tea,
What a lovely moment for Margaret, her fan, to keep in her memory.
Our noble monarch is so full of grace and reigns supreme,
We all salute Her Majesty, our most gracious Queen.
So to a wonderful lady, this message we would like to relay,
Hope, Your Royal Highness rules for many a long day.
So Ma'am, we stand and raise our glasses to you,
And toast to your health, happiness and long life too.

God bless you.

S Kinsey

Elizabeth Regina

The spirit of love is dancing across the palace grounds
Amidst the bouquet of good wishes
A gracious rose of hope may be found
Elizabeth Regina
Overflowing grace in all you say and do
The gatekeeper of memory, true love a nation's gift to you
We unlock the book of memory deep within our hearts
Unfold so many moments of which you are a part
May a symphony of love, happiness and joy trace your way
Elizabeth Regina
We salute a gracious sovereign on this, your special day

Maureen Boyd Joines Anderson

Sonnet On The Queen's Birthday
(For Queen Elizabeth II)

The second of your line, but greater in peace
And wartime than the first one of that name;
Having across many years shown to us more grace,
And steadiness of heart - a constant flame
Of dutiful concern - both as gentle wife,
And as compliant daughter. Equally at home
Among your people, as Queen; accepting of pain and grief,
With flowery face and unexampled calm;
A mother also of fair children, every one
Enriched by you - as we are, all of us.
May you live long, to grace our English throne.
With English virtues, with a bright smiling face,
For what you were and are, engages us now,
As does your smile, as beautiful as snow.

Alan C Brown

The Queen

I admire the Queen,
I know what she's been,
The light of my life,
As she was a
Great wife,
A lady of survival,
Making life able,
Travelling and living,
Happiness to the
Queen, she has
Long been.

Barbara Brown

Lilibet At 80

The Queen at 80, well where to start?
I must write her a poem that comes from the heart.
With the death of her father after years of ill health,
A pretty young girl was now Head of State and the Commonwealth.
She would lead the nation and lead us with pride,
With her young man Philip, to help at her side.
A nation recovering from a war and the Blitz,
We would look to this woman, we loved her to bits.
It wouldn't be long before Charles came to the fore,
Then Ann, then Andy, then Edward. Blimey that's four!
Princes and princess would be seen playing with Mummy,
So the Royals are like us, well isn't that funny.
As the years went by, certain milestones she'd reach,
Christmas Day at three we would gather to watch the Queen's speech.
When the nations had suffered, she suffered too,
And when you suffered Ma'am we suffered with you.
How many hands have you shaken at home and abroad?
How many trips have you taken? You must never get bored.
And now you are 80 and look happy and so well,
With your family around you, what stories you must tell.
Well you're the best monarch that we have ever seen,
So happy birthday Your Majesty and God save the Queen.

Geoff Donkin

Gracious Queen

Our Queen of many happy years
Mixed with sad ones that have brought forth tears
Throughout them all you have been strong and calm
Imbuing all your subjects with your healing balm
Oh, good and gracious Queen
In your life you've reigned serene
As a young princess in a world at war
Where you led we followed and gave up more
Majesty, while you sit upon your throne
Do you think of your subjects as your own?
Do you plan your day with us in mind?
And in your heart are you honest and kind?
Do you feel that your reign is a crushing bore
And that your duties are just an endless chore?
What is in your mind as you ride on your horse?
Do you think your corgis are a tour de force?
When your birthday comes round do you, like us,
Exclaim excitedly and be thrilled at the fuss?
Do you remember your life back to when you were small
When you knew what you wanted with no trouble at all?
Well, in this bountiful country that is ours
We know we don't want gifts or bunches of flowers
We just want peace and in your eightieth year
Just thank God for His gift of a Queen sincere.

Royston E Herbert

Elizabeth, Crowned Queen In 1953

Elizabeth Alexandra Mary
beautiful grandmother,
Queen of our hearts,
she shines like no other.

Choirboys are sending
songs of praise her way,
on twenty-first of April,
her eightieth birthday.

She is the sweet Queen,
and we thank God above;
with modesty she rules
this green land we love.

People of our kingdom
and over sand and sea,
pay homage to Elizabeth
our gracious deity.

National events with
the 'red, white and blue'
are too many to mention,
they'd reach to the moon.

Yet she has been there
with dedication true,
the Duke of Edinburgh beside her,
helping her through.

She's 'happy and glorious'
she is surely victorious;
on the twenty-first April
God bless Her Majesty.

Joyce Hemsley

Happy Birthday, Your Majesty!

In nineteen twenty-six, it's true,
Before the world knew some of you,
Elizabeth, a princess fair,
Was born to become the royal heir.

80 years - a great milestone
For the Queen we call our own.
She reigns for you, she reigns for me.
Happy birthday, Your Majesty!

She's shared our hopes, she's shared our fears,
Through the many rolling years.
In spite of all the change that came,
Our sovereign still remains the same.

She's proved a conscientious Queen,
How fortunate this land has been.
God grant that she may know His will,
Serving the folk that love her still.

We pray for wisdom from above
To help her rule in truth and love,
The nation to which we belong,
Sounding forth this grateful song!

So join with us to celebrate
This one who helps make Britain great,
A monarch o'er the years adored,
May she reign for many more!

Matthew Pickhaver

Happy Birthday

This ageless time of age
is written on many a page
for you look the same today
as in many a yesterday
your timeless grace prevails
and your beauty never pales
yet your ageless wisdom grows
as all who meet you knows
that time with you is rare
but a joy for all to share
and in the greatness of your life
you're a mother, queen and wife
a friend, yet uniquely royal
hard-working, compassionate, loyal
you give each of us a share
of your wisdom, grace and care
so we thank you then today
and wish you the best ever birthday.

Daphne Cornell

The Queen

God bless the Queen
Her reign has been
One to make us proud.

She's fulfilled her call
And served us all
As she long ago vowed.

Never shirking her task
She's all we could ask
How fortunate we've been

She's our pride and gain
Long, long may she reign
God save the Queen.

Pat Wearn

For You

Like a soldier you march,
With strength and passion as your guide,
Like the tallest flower
Which refuses to bow in the battering wind.
You show what grace is,
The strength and spirit of a nation.

You were every young girl's dream,
The reputation and tradition of a nation,
Forged by your line
Is now carried and maintained by your shoulders.
You are the strength and spirit of our nation.
Our Queen.

Samantha Douglas

Lady Of Britain

The years have flown by
and gathered a whole array of memories
times have been difficult
but you overcame them
glorious memories are instilled within you
how it must feel, so wonderful to be you
how privileged you have been
to own the country and title as Queen
how your mannerisms have been ascertained
throughout the many decades of your whole being
to travel the seas
and step on the grasses so green
to feel the power of war
in all its upset and blood pour
to relate to young and old
to feel a part of the family
to love your pets as you do
to be the Queen
is a living dream.

R Pang

Birthday Greetings

Your 80 years have seen much change
Once empire proud where sun ne'er set
When Duke of York took over throne
Acknowledged king in London Town.

Wartime came - evacuees
Warmed to your broadcast giving hope
With Margaret Rose you wished them well
Away from danger of the Blitz.

Those post-war years of endless grey
Were brightened up by wedding bells
Many flocked to Abbey steps
Catching glimpse of bride and groom.

Then heady coronation times
The fifties dawned - another age
A wind of change for better things
Before the sixties' swinging scene.

I could go on to fill a book
Of people, places - foreign shores
Touching thousands with your smile
Something special in their lives.

So now I send my kind regards
Expressed in verse - a loyal bouquet
What milestone! - Shared by one and all
Enjoy your happy, happy day!

Steve Glason

In Praise Of Our Queen

A lady of substance,
A lady of charm,
Her reign has seen changes,
She has remained calm.
Groomed to perfection
Whenever she's seen
We admire and respect you
Elizabeth, our Queen.

In stature she is tiny
Her mentality strong
Perceptive, her vision
Sees right from wrong.
A wry sense of humour
Fun-loving too
Happy birthday, dear Majesty
Is what we wish you.

Still lovely at eighty,
Skin fine as lace
A smile like sunshine,
Lights up her face.
Adored by her family
A mother and wife.
May God bless our Queen
In the fullness of life.

Pamela Carder

Royal Visit In The Rain

The school was buzzing with excitement,
Her Majesty was coming to town,
Happy children with many questions,
Would Queen Elizabeth wear her crown?

The purpose of the royal visit,
Was to see our design guide new town
And to plant a tree in the centre,
Despite the rain pouring down!

How thrilled we were that special day,
When the news came that the royal car
Would drive past our new primary school,
To give us a chance to shout 'Hurrah!'

Children dressed in their uniforms,
Lined the pavement outside the school,
And I nervously made doubly sure
That no one was acting the fool.

We waited patiently in the rain,
As minutes slowly ticked away.
We got wetter with each new shower,
But the excitement was there to stay.

At last the royal car appeared,
It stopped right outside the school gate,
All the children began to cheer,
And I knew it had been worth the wait.

Two children presented a bouquet,
And a card designed by Class Two,
The Queen smiled with appreciation,
And the bubble of excitement grew.

At last Her Majesty went on her way,
But I won't forget that perfect day.

Doreen M Bowers

A Contemporary Salutes Her Majesty On Her Eightieth Birthday

You symbolise the country that we love,
In your own person bear our history.
In your veins run the tributary streams
Of Celtic, Roman, Saxon, Norman blood,
That confluence which made us what we are.
And when I see you now, your face set
With duty's burdens, I remember how you were
In girlhood's prime, those testing wartime years,
Before a heavy crown had crushed your curls,
Wearing not royal blue, but drab khaki,
Like millions more, your fellow citizens,
Who, in grim unity, withstood the threat
Hurled at them from the innocent summer skies.
Or see you speaking to a microphone
Your girlish resolution, even then,
To do what God willed, love and serve
Your country and its people. And I see
That sad day when, in mourning veiled
For a loved father, you stepped out of a plane
To hear, for the first time, the fateful words,
'Your Majesty' and knew how God had called.
But after mourning rose that glorious day
When my agnostic heart thrilled to hear
The choir's ringing anthem as you moved
With slow solemnity towards the throne,
'Regina! Regina! Regina!' Then the shout
Triumphant of 'Long live the Queen'.
So all the nation rises echoing,
'A happy birthday, Ma'am, long may you reign,
And England live to be her own green self again.'

Jim Morgan

The Queen

I have a friend - American
Who comes to visit me
A man, proud of his country
And so the man should be.

He talks about his vast land
The beauty to be seen
I say, 'We may be smaller,
But we have got the Queen.'

While you may fill your garden
Ten times with my small plot
You may be proud of many things
That I just haven't got.

I cross my land in hours
For you, it may take days
And yet our lives are tied up
In very many ways.

But one thing that you don't have
And you'll know what I mean
Be proud of your America
But I have got the Queen.

Gordon Andrews

Poem To The Queen

You are such an inspiration
And someone to admire
For your loyalty and devotion
That never seems to tire

Long may you reign Your Majesty
For we're very proud to tell
You're a very special lady
Who has served our country well

Sylvia Dyer

Happy Birthday, Your Majesty

Queen Elizabeth II, happy birthday to you,
You're so dedicated in all that you do,
I like your speeches at Christmas time,
And I must say, you deliver them fine.

You've led the country well, since your coronation,
I pray for yours and our families' salvation,
That God will be merciful to each one of them,
Especially those who are not born again.

I enjoyed your trips on the royal yacht,
Showing places where you'd been and I had not,
Your colour of outfits are all so supreme,
Praise be to God, you're a wonderful Queen.

Your Majesty is eighty years young,
And the birthday song, the loudest ever sung,
I hope and pray you have many, many more,
Although not as many as you had before.

Samuel McAlister

The Queen's 80th Birthday

The Queen's a stability to England
and does the job with pride,
the corgis are always well groomed
and by her side.
Her dedication to her work is done well
with pride.
Her horses are a pride to be seen,
and her guards are a lovely sight
everything about her palace
is a glory to the Queen.
God bless you today on your special day,
may happiness be with you all day.
Happy birthday, Your Majesty.

D McDonald

Eighty Glorious Years

On a wet and dreary April morn
A lovely little girl was born.
Not in a royal palace or castle
But in a London Mayfair house.

At just thirteen she fell in love
With a dashing young cadet.
At twenty-one she wed that handsome sailor
A marriage made in Heaven above.

The young and happy, loving couple
Were known far and wide.
When in Kenya her beloved father died
A sad homecoming for our beloved Queen.

Throughout her long and gracious lifetime
She has served the nation well.
Dedicated to the commonwealth
Admired and respected everywhere.

In her illustrious lifetime
She has known much change and sorrow.
Meet her every need oh Lord
And guide her evermore.

Now as eighty years have passed
She has fulfilled a heavy task.
We salute our Sovereign Lady
God bless and keep her in Your care.

Georgina Johnston

April 21, 2006

What radiance and joy,
Warmth and happiness in abundance,
Overflowing.
Our gracious Queen
In vibrant fuchsia,
A vision of beauty.
Simplicity and style,
Natural response
- A sense of intimacy
As everyone watched and joined in
- A walkabout,
Where exuberance and happy faces beamed,
Excited children danced on the kerbside,
Crowds patiently waited and responded.
Tears of joy
As music added to the moment
- Cherished by her people,
Admiring and loving
Every moment,
Tangible and historic,
Personal and heart-warming.
The Queen and Prince Philip
Touched our hearts
And enabled us to say,
'Thank you and happy birthday.'

Margaret Ann Wheatley

God Bless The Queen At Eighty

We see the ceremony and the pomp
some distance off, though zoomed by camera lens
into our living rooms. A right royal romp
in gold and scarlet trappings. Women's, men's
and children's raiments, livery of all styles
competes with guardsmen's uniforms for praise.
The ambience enhanced by gleaming smiles
lends light to this so special day of days.
You've lived through four score years, faithfully served
for more than half a century as our Queen;
through highs and lows you've never been unnerved,
so steadfast in your vows, so calm, serene.
Stability is what this country owes you.
You well deserve the fealty it shows you.

Adrian Brett

She Rules With Grace

Loved by kind folk, big and small,
She is known to one and all,
Calm and cool, she has a style,
The whole world has seen that smile,
A light to all, creed or race,
Then and now, she rules with grace.

Keep the faith and speak with pride,
Spread the good word, far and wide,
This day, the day of her birth,
It is time, for joy and mirth,
Make your wish and raise a cheer,
Say it soft but say it clear,

It will be, as it has been,
All hearts join, to bless, the Queen.

Ken Lou

Jubilant Heart Of Oak

80 years she's been on this Earth,
A queen of outstanding worth.
So much has happened, some bad, but more good,
But a monarch of strength she has always stood.

The media, in vain, tried with all their ploys,
To underestimate the loyalty she enjoys.
To bring about a fallen throne,
Ignorant of its foundation of solid stone.

Millions of subjects can't be wrong,
Our monarchy will remain, forever strong.
Who in the media served a fifty-year term?
Yet Elizabeth has, will they never learn?

God Save our Queen's not just a song on the whole,
But words of our prayers to a much higher soul.
Now if He's seen fit to keep her secure,
Then who's our guide? Not the media, I'm sure.

John Worthington

I'd Love To Meet The Queen

I'd love to meet the Queen
But I probably never will.
A trip to England costs so much,
But it sure would be a thrill.
And maybe I could talk to her,
But I'm not sure what I'd say.
There's not much we have in common,
But I'd like to meet her anyway.
And maybe we'd be on TV,
But would I look good on the screen?
It would be a great adventure,
But I'll probably never meet the Queen.

Jay Berkowitz

Let Us Show

Her Majesty, the Queen
Loves universal peace
Her Majesty, the Queen
Loves the human race
In commemoration
Of the Queen's 80th birthday
Let us all pledge,
Yes . . .
We shall forever
Coexist in peace,
To show our solidarity.
Shower brotherhood,
To show our unity.
Protect our environs,
To show our concern.
Vow for social awakening,
To show our might.
Strive to uplift the poor,
To show humane instinct.
Provide succour to the needy,
To define human nature.
Provide shelter to the orphans,
To show our warmth.
Impart peace,
To show our trust.
Render humane service,
To show our concern for all.
Restore friendship bonds,
To show our trust.
Shun violent motives,
To show our goodwill.

Ashok Chakravarthy

Elizabethan Ages

Two great Elizabethan ages -
Two queens devoted to their country,
Whose coronations were the start
Of glorious years for all their subjects.

The first encouraged exploits from men who strove
To glorify her name and bring enrichment to this land.
Admiral Sir Francis Drake who circumnavigated the world
And brought about the great defeat of Spanish vessels
Threatening the peace of this, her realm.
Explorer, writer, beloved of his queen,
Sir Walter Raleigh sailed to unknown shores
Bringing back knowledge of America's vast lands.
The unknown world was opening up before her eyes,
While from Will Shakespeare's pen great literary works now flowed.

A young and lovely queen - a second Queen Elizabeth,
And many prophesied a second golden age.
Across the wide world her dominions spread
While she herself could travel far and wide
To visit places unknown centuries ago.
No longer wooden sailing ships but great grey metal monsters,
With submarines beneath the waves and aircraft overhead.
Sound barrier broken, nuclear power and men upon the moon,
Undreamt of in the sixteenth century.

We thank her for her leadership, her good example,
A constant in this troubled world of curse.
Though tragedy and worries have at times beset her,
She never falters in her service to us all.
Long may she live - the ruler of this second glorious age.

Roma Davies

HRH Queen Elizabeth II - Eighty Years Young

Hail to thee Elizabeth II
Your treasured smile
Is our inherited wealth
And your beautiful possession
In picture or in person

Little we know
How the years at gallop flow
Leaving a trail to sow
The seeds of harmony

Eighty years young
And may God bring you
Another twenty-one
To sail and soothe the tides
On the sea of tranquillity

God bless Elizabeth II.

Jean Bald

Her Royal Highness The Queen At Eighty

The queen is eighty this year
the year two thousand and six
looking so youthful with so much to bear
with a huge hat full of ideas and tricks

her complexion so fair and radiant
a bright sparkle in her eyes
with all her make-up adumbrate
as she waves gloved handed with farewells and goodbyes

her remembered styles and dresses from occasions past
events attended with presents and flowers
places she's visited and castles that last
shoes and umbrellas for sunshine and showers

we hope she's around for many more years
there will be tears and disappointment when she disappears

Gina A Miller

Queen Elizabeth II

Always regal, rules supreme
Elizabeth II, our wonderful Queen.

Devoted, majestic, never tiring
Kind and thoughtful, always inspiring.

Born to rule, a privileged position
A life chosen for a special mission.

You radiate warmth with your charm and grace
Kindness shines forth from your gentle face.

Proud and glorious
Royal and serene
Elizabeth II
Our wonderful Queen.

Christine Hardemon

Untitled

Majesty and dignity
Strong in adversity
Her grace is plain to see
In our Queen

And we give our applause
At home and abroad
We give thanks to God
For our Queen

Her charm still never fades
Now after eight decades
So we give our accolade
To our Queen!

Barbara Collar

Year Of The Disabled

Anne and I were invited to a garden party
In the grounds of Buckingham Palace
It was to do with the year of the disabled
We were thrilled when the invitations
Dropped on the doormat, then the big day came
And dressed in our Sunday best
We set off along the A1
The sun was shining as we entered The Mall
We drove through Buckingham Palace gates
Oh what a thrill, we felt like royalty
We strolled down to the lake
Then the heavens opened
So into the marquee for our tea
Once it faired up the royal party made an appearance
The Queen, Prince Philip, Princess Anne, Prince Charles
And as she was then Lady Diana
All mingled with the guests
The Queen asked Anne, 'Where's your husband?'
'Behind me, Ma'am,' came the answer.
Prince Philip told Anne, 'Your wheelchair will go rusty
In the rain'
There were a few guide dogs
And I heard Prince Philip say
'It's like a dog show here today'
Then back home a day to remember
The only regret because of the wheelchair
We couldn't go through the palace, no ramp.

Richard Trowbridge

Our Sovereign Queen

A lady first but one of many
revered by her nation this anniversary
such demeanour and majestic carriage
a sparkling example of a perfect marriage

Years have matured her stunning style
knowing expression was once girlish smile
head held high with twinkling eye
such an example of strength for you and I

One century past, and this one present
what future looms, what effervescence
this nation strides as strong and sure
to help steer the international ship to shore

Stern times would lie ahead but she
has mothered one to lead us still free
surety, strength and historically bred
in the steps of royal characters he will tread

Loyalty has been our strength, this country
held in awe by many a foreign society
now in this age of modern technicality
a leading voice promotes example with heraldry

A lady last for she has been
such fine example of a modern Queen
we do so revere her stately grandeur
and wish for ourselves that Her Majesty endure.

Peter G Hoar

80th Birthday Wish For Queen Elizabeth

I wrote a poem,
just like any other,
except this one was special
it was about your mother.

You were married on 20th November
and I was born the next day after.
I am named Elizabeth too,
my mother named me after you.

I have followed you . . .
on all your occasions
and remember very well,
your coronation.

You have stood up, firm and true,
in everything you have had to do,
all through the good times, bad times too,
I know your mother was proud of you.

So I am writing this poem, just for you,
to let you know, you are thought of too.
So, Ma'am, enjoy this, your day of 'plenty',
as you reach the age of 'eighty'.
Many happy returns, Your Royal Highness.

Elizabeth Anne Gifford

Birthday Bonus

Special events merit celebrations,
Personal or national, important occasions.
Birthdays, weddings, graduations, successes,
Unique opportunities, as each day marks steady progress.

Lambs leaping enthusiastically on a spring day,
Flowers a-peeping through earth and clay.
Birds with fledglings attempting to fly,
Babes newly born, announcing life with a cry.

As years pass by, changing scenes
Contribute to growth on healthy green.
Growing in stature, wisdom and strength,
April's now here, when we remember Her Majesty's birth.

We join together with good wishes and praise
For the one who ably copes during passing phases.
Subjects expressing homage, as she continues to smile,
To an honourable monarch, who walks in style.

Easter time we commemorate, and is a reminder of new life,
Second birthday of the Saviour, God's Son, Jesus Christ.
He arose triumphant, thus enabling humanity to celebrate
                                        spiritual birth,
Walking beside us, supplying blessing and strength, today and always.

A R Harcus

Our Queen

C ongratulations, Ma'am, to you
O n every aspect of your reign,
R egarding with integrity
G reat Britain's past in human gain.
I n everything you show the way

B y doing just the best you can,
A nd though you sometimes feel dismay
R egarding all your queenly chores,
K ennels of corgis witness here
S o much we owe to you and yours.
   Our heartfelt barks!

C M Pountney

Untitled

Our Queen rules like an angel,
And equals any saint.
Great burdens has she shouldered,
Would make some people faint.
Her smiles and all her beauty,
Are like an English rose,
Happy birthday, Ma'am, you're eighty
And reached your golden years,
So all your loyal subjects,
Applaud their golden cheers,
And wish you lots of happiness,
For your future reigning years.

K M Abbott

Happy Birthday, Ma'am

On twenty-first of April 1926
Way before I was born
A young princess came into the world
A joyous and happy morn

Elizabeth by name, royal by birth
Duty and service she pledged
Jubilees silver and golden too
She does what she does best

Heads of state, prime ministers galore
She's had them all to tea
Visits to the Commonwealth by plane and ship
Britannia ruled the sea

Fun and merriment, pomp and ceremony
The Trooping of the Colour
The opening of Parliament, in regal gown
Royal Ascot. Did she back the winner?

Currency and stamps, mugs and teatowels
She's never far from view
And the latest portrait of the many dozens
Rolf's in beautiful turquoise hue

Two birthdays a year, Royal Variety shows
Garden parties for the lucky
The Christmas Day speech, New Year's honours too
My goodness she is kept busy

Trials and tribulations, dignified and strong
Her Majesty remains steadfast
Happy birthday, Ma'am, on your eighty years
Our affections in stone are cast

Anne Marie Latham

To A Royal Octogenarian

Behind the ceremonial pomp
There shines a human face
A kindly tale despite the veil
Of dignity and grace;
We know you danced the conga
With the crowd, so long ago,
But blithe display must needs give way
To inner radiant glow -
The burden of affairs of state,
Traditions to preserve,
Sometimes, perhaps, you wonder
'Does a monarch reign or serve?'
Yet, in an ever-changing world,
You play a steadfast role -
A vibrant living symbol
Of the nation's heart and soul!
It gives us joy to celebrate
Your long, devoted life -
A trusty, shining beacon
As a mother, Queen and wife.

Desmond Quick

Felicitations

Of one whose royal regal power emblazoned worldwide
Reigning with God's guidance as with His holy words abide
As we celebrate a birthday and pay tributes far and wide
To Elizabeth, our Queen, so admired with pride
'Happy birthday, Ma'am'
Loyal and sincere throughout though many stresses no doubt?
Conquering these strains that brought about
Your gracious charm held all enthralled
Speechless as you are continually adored
Now on this day our respects all pay
As many unite and pray may this be one of the most happiest of days
A 'happy birthday, Ma'am'.

R D Hiscoke

Birthday Congratulations

Your Majesty, I send heartfelt good wishes
To add to those from far and near
I hope you enjoy the many celebrations
In this, your 80th birthday year

I remember when I was a little girl aged nine
Watching with the rest of the nation
As the golden coach carried you
To Westminster Abbey for your coronation

Your life is so very hectic
Lots of places to go and people to see
No doubt sometimes all you feel like doing
Is sitting with your feet up with a nice cup of tea

I know you and your family have often visited
The beautiful Lake District which is where I live
I feel sure you did enjoy the time you spent
In this area which has so much to give

So I raise a glass and give three cheers
To add to the birthday scene
And wish continued good health and happiness
To you, Ma'am, our much loved Queen

Jackie Richardson

Untitled

Her Maj is really great,
Never late for an important date,
Looks so good, really nice,
Very important, like sugar and spice,
We all love her, especially too,
More than ever, she knows we do,
She's good for the British and the land,
That's why she makes the perfect ma'am.

Lorraine Fisher

A Sovereign Lady

Her Majesty, Queen Elizabeth the Second,
Rules so graciously, yet life must have beckoned
Her to step down, to lay aside her crown,
Kick up her heels, let her hair down.
Instead she has chosen to willingly perform
Her duties with dignity and decorum
In the role which is the envy of the world
With its pageantry with banners unfurled,
And the ancient traditions and heraldry.
What more pleasing sights could one ever see?
The Queen riding in the Trooping of the Colour
Is a very special event, unlike any other,
To which people from countries far and wide
Travel eagerly to view this unique parade.
As a princess she played her part in the war
Helping to keep the enemy from our shore;
Wearing the uniform of the ATS,
In her father's army she stood the test.
She has been our head for many, many years,
As an ambassadress for us she has no peers.
Throughout history there has never been
A sovereign more regal than our Queen;
She has high ideals, has never set a foot wrong,
'God Save The Queen', we regale her with song.

Marlene Allen

The Crown Of Royal Duty

A smile that lights up your face,
A sense of humour, charm, grace,
Wisdom, responsibility, strength,
A reign of enduring length,
Bearing the awesome crown of royal duty,
With a dignified beauty.

M J Harris

A Job For Life
(A rondeau for the occasion of Her Majesty's 80th birthday)

A job for life - yes, just as Elizabeth I, you, dear
Queen will reign; a nation applauds your worthy cause; here
In the hearts of your people, now as you near the close
We congratulate you, our sovereign lady; from those
First crowned days in 1953; let's give a hearty cheer!

Elizabeth II, you have done a good job, and may your sheer
Elegance, grandeur and beauty - plus good sense, see
You through to your goal, to carry on, and be the best - our rose
A job for life.

You have taken the rough with the smooth, through many a year
With family problems, as many others do; but no matter what fear
Trouble or woe - a smiling face you always show; only
                                        goodness knows
How you, great lady, in the years to come - will succeed, win and bear
A job for life.

Valerie Hall

A Tribute To Her Majesty

Her Majesty is eighty, she has now reached her four score
And she still looks amazing, like she's fit for twenty more!
She's followed in the footsteps of a famous dynasty
And she's carried out her duties with grace and dignity.
She's lived her life in a goldfish bowl of world publicity
And through it all she's shown a face of calm serenity.
She's had to weather many storms within her family,
And she has had to cope with domestic tragedy.
She's always been the living proof of Britishness at its best
To overcome adversity with a smile and a jest.
She is admired throughout the world wherever she is known
And we know we are fortunate to have her for our own.
There are no words that can convey our love and gratitude
To our very special Queen who's reigned with fortitude.

Elizabeth Monk

Elizabeth II

A wonderful Queen,
so courteous and kind.
So stately serene,
a wonderful mind.

Whatever you have seen,
some good, some bad.
Always a smile,
perhaps feeling sad.

A life of devotion,
to a job well done.
Showing no emotion,
if things are wrong.

A tribute to you,
long may you reign.
May God be with you,
whatever you do.

Thora Carpenter

Sent From A Distance

accept, dear Queen, Her Majesty
the gift, a token gift
you might never look out for

and like green leave, greening in spring
you're richer in that than I am
who in silence had read a world
in time aperture
travelling through same route of life

and be like kid again
I send you
therefore
a gift of smile unasked -
and of amour . . .

Felix Oriseikwe Sylvanus

A Royal Pageant

William the Conqueror started it all with his lifelong ambition to be
Ruler of Anglo Saxon lands on an island across the sea.

Poor Harold was slain with an arrow it's said and his army just
    turned round and ran
This was the start of a new royal house and the Norman
    lineage began.

William Rufus and Henry I, King Stephen became the next bet
But he had no offspring so over from France came Henry Plantagenet.

Richard I was followed by John but his attitude was a non-starter
And so he was forced by his lords to sign the infamous Magna Carta.

Four Henrys, five Edwards then all took their turn with one Richard
    in-between
Until Richard III brought it all to an end at the Battle of Bosworth scene.

Two Henrys, an Edward and Mary I all tasted the Tudor crown
Then good Queen Bess took over the reigns until Scotland sent
    King James down.

The Stuart lineage continued with Charles, who managed to lose
    his head
Then Oliver Cromwell jumped in his shoes as soon as poor Charles
    was dead.

Charly II came back to rule for the blood in his veins was blue
And when his merry life came to an end he was followed by James
    number two.

William and Mary then came along, followed by good Queen Anne
And she was the last of the Stuart house and the Hanoverians began.

Four Georges, a William and Victoria too, all helped to make
    Great Britain great
Until Edward VII took over command, albeit a little bit late.

And so the House of Windsor was born and we had a new family tree
With two Georges, an Edward and Lilibet too, who became
    Her Majesty.

The pageant continues to this very day, an ever-changing scene
God bless these islands and God bless our realm and God bless
    our gracious Queen.

Denise Castellani

Her Royal Smile

The royal family were on walkabout.

I did not expect to see any of them - what with such vast crowds and being only 5ft tall!

The atmosphere was wonderful.
People in the front rows excitedly gave those further back a rundown of what was taking place.

We heard that the Queen was heading in our direction,
along with Princes William and Harry.

There was Her Majesty!

The crowds seemed to divide - like the parting of the Red Sea.
Her smile so radiant.

I returned the smile
while going into complete shock.

Now, I had seen both mother and daughter close-up.
Previously, Princess Anne, now the Queen.

What a wonderful day!

A day to remember, where sadness and joy complemented each other,
at this, the opening of the Princess Diana Memorial in Hyde
                                        Park, London.

Cheryl Campbell

Meeting Of The Minds

Are we going to the palace, will the Queen be home for tea?
Put your coat and hat on, dear, we'll have to wait and see.
Will the guards be there protecting her, sentries on the gate?
Tie your other shoelace, dear, do hurry, we'll be late.
Will everyone be cheering if she goes out for a ride?
Just turn your head a little while I adjust your slide.
Will we see her princes and her princesses too?
Before we go now promise me you'll go and use the loo.
What about her husband and her corgi dogs?
Don't run and trip today dear, you'll ruin your new togs.
Will she wear her crown d'you think, and her ermine cape?
I really wish I'd made your bows out of Grandma's crepe.
Will she ride her favourite horse or travel in a coach?
I think that coat you're wearing could do with a small brooch.
I wonder if her arm aches as she waves to all the crowd.
Oh, you do look wonderful, you make me feel right proud.
Is she as old as Grandma, is eighty really old?
Now just you watch your ps and qs and mind what you've been told.
Do you think she'll still be Queen when I reach eighty-eight?
Now take my hand, mind that step, that's it, just shut the gate.
Will she have a special meal and a great big birthday cake?
Don't forget your seat belt dear in case I have to brake.
Dad says she's our ambassador for all the world to see.
That's right, she is and a better one I'll bet you'll never see.

Win Tipson

A Poem For Her Majesty

Elizabeth II, God truly save our gracious Queen
Bejewelled, dignified, majestic and serene

It's your 80th year but you're still going strong
You've given your life to your country for so very long

The saddest day long ago meant you would dedicate
Your all to our island to make Britain *Great!*

Not just our monarch - wife, mum and grandmother
You've reigned and served us like no other

Just like us, you've had some difficult years
But you've always managed to smile through your tears

Never seen to complain or use the fact that you're royalty
Like the trooper you are, you've always done your duty

You must have wished sometimes you could have stayed in bed
But unlike many, you continued to work instead!

Some may think: riches, castles and jewels
But I know it's hard work and they are just fools!

Each Christmas you grace our screens with your speech
You show us you care and are not out of reach

I was so excited last July, an invitation arrived for me
It was the Queen's pleasure to invite me for tea!

Mum's charity work was the source of this request
And I was lucky enough to be her guest!

The dress code was strict and security was tight
But seeing the tourists watching us was such a delight!

We ate delicious sandwiches and sweet little cakes
Then walked around the pretty grounds and lakes

Then Her Majesty arrived and we stood for the anthem
But there were so many guests, catching a glimpse was a problem!

Well that was a day to remember and I'll raise a glass of champagne
A toast on her 80th birthday *and* long may she reign!

Beverley R Stepney

Our Queen

I was just a baby when you first did reign
The glorious throne which you did claim
And rightly so, as over the years
You've shown your love for us and served
With pride in our country, the Commonwealth too
Oh precious Queen, your people are so proud of you
Through many anniversaries and the children you have born
You've been through many stages in your life, some your heart
has torn
But your precious people hold you high
And will forever do so until the day is nigh
You're 80 now, my, how time has flown
And in these precious years your majesty has grown
May this special year bring you happy times so gay
As to you, these special words, I have to say
You'll always be our Queen, we cherish you in every way.

Maggie Strong

Poem For The Queen

This poem for our Queen who is always serene
Has regally ruled with an air so supreme.
The dignity of you, Ma'am, when times are bad
Maintaining your demeanour even when sad.
You never have faltered in your reign
When the world around you is becoming insane.
You love your Scotland with all the heather
You can lose yourself in the dramatic weather.
At times you must pine for your beloved canine
But Susan is waiting for you in another time.
The people love you because you are proud
'God save the Queen' we sing out loud.
So many happy returns to our sovereign true
Birthday greetings and wishes we send to you.
Eighty years young and long may you stay
To enjoy your great grandchildren at work and play.

Sarah Scott

Our Queen

I am sitting in my garden wondering what to write,
With garden friends is such a delight.
I was listening to the radio, I think the BBC,
That informed me the Queen was nearly eighty.
It is hard to imagine, for the years have flown so fast,
For you, our Queen, it is a busy task.
I remember on your journey from childhood to inner youth,
You explored so many tasks with you family roots.
But how the years have passed and busy Ma'am you have been,
Travelling all over the Commonwealth, as our English Queen.
And in-between manoeuvres still busy as can be,
You had Charles, Anne, Andrew and Edward, the perfect family.
Still attending to matter, to country and world alike,
You brought up a family with the Duke by your side.
Has to be special having family about,
Like any family it has its ups and downs,
The trouble, Ma'am, is you wear the crown.
I often criticise the TV and press,
For never allowing the royals to rest.
I am sitting in my garden saying a special prayer,
To thank you, dear Ma'am, for you and being there.
You are our monarchy and doing extremely well,
As I look at all the memories and do dwell.
A chapter ending, a new one to start,
Exciting happenings to you I impart.
I'll send a special blessing to God, Queen and country,
I am a loyal subject and that's how I always am.
England, dear England, a queen or king I will always see
And always give homage and true identity.

Carol Bernadette Boneham

Queen Elizabeth

Your Majesty, our gracious Queen
Elizabeth, on your 80th birthday
We thank you for your years of service
To us, your loyal subjects.
For all the years you have served us
We are full of thanks and praise.
For your devotions to duty, service and kindness
In good times visiting to encourage and rejoice
To sympathise in times of loss and trouble.
For your devotions to duty we thank you,
Your Christian faith is an example to all.
Year by year when skies are blue
And when trouble comes along,
For your example and devotion to duty
We thank and praise God for you.
For your family - The Duke of Edinburgh,
Your children and grandchildren,
Balancing time for your family,
England, the empire and Commonwealth too
We thank God for you all.
For welcoming heads of state
And for travelling to distant lands,
Always cheerful with the right words to say:
For your devotion to duty in all circumstances
We thank God for you and your family too.

Jean Martin-Doyle

Our Queen Elizabeth II

She is our Queen - the Head of State
She took on the task at an early age.
She did not ask for this estate but
She inherited the job which was her fate.
She married a prince who gave her support
She had four children - her rules she taught
Like her mother before her, she watched them grow
Into individuals with different woes.
She loved her mother who gave good advice
She too had been a remarkable wife.
She did her duty as wife, mother and Queen and
She served her country for the whole of her life.
She lived by strong principles during her reign
And by never complaining, and never explained.
This helped her to live as a much honoured Queen
And she reached the age of 80 years and
Reigned supreme - God bless her.

Doris E Pullen

Greetings - Elizabeth II

Who is the Elizabeth that we see,
So gracious in her majesty.
She's steadfast in duty, dignified,
Respected in Britain and worldwide.

Her manner, decorum, does not show
Who is Elizabeth, hidden below.
One can only guess at the hidden soul
Of Queen of England, acting her role.

She's a mortal thrust into public life
With normal duties of family and wife.
She's a clever juggler, now at eighty,
Managing her privacy.

Pauline Boncey

Queen Elizabeth's Birthday

To the royal garden party,
Behind the gates of iron,
The royal beasts were invited,
Both unicorn and lion.

Children were wearing fancy dress,
From books, films or DVDs,
From nursery rhymes and fairy tales,
Indeed, anything that would please.

Alice in Wonderland was there,
Harry Potter from Hogwarts,
All faithfully represented,
Celebrities of all sorts.

There were clever entertainers,
Things to drink and things to eat,
All kinds of music was playing,
Reaching the ears and feet.

Wishing 'Many happy returns',
To our present reigning Queen,
Memories of good times gone by,
With new times yet to be seen.

Kathleen M Scatchard

A Poem To My Queen On Her Birthday! (Yay!)

Hello my Queen of beauty and proud,
I think everyone knows you all around,
I look up to you as if my idol,
But obviously I cannot be as I'm not royalty,
But as you hopefully know I would love to!
You make me so happy when I see and hear you!
You even cheer me up when I hear your lovely voice!
I wish you the very best of luck on this special day!
Long live our victorious Queen.
Happy birthday, lovely Queen!

Mathilda Lucas-Box (12)

Long May She Reign

There was rain on the day I first saw her
A snowy picture on a tiny screen
As neighbours filled Mrs Johnson's back room
June 2nd 1953 - I was five.

There was rain the next time I saw her.
Schoolchildren lined a processional route
Waiting, sodden, dripping, cold
As the car sped past and a gloved hand waved.

There was rain on that awful day in Windsor
Feverish with cold, she watched her castle burn
But more unkind than accidental flames
An uncaring people who refused to pay.

A constant in my life is how I view her
An integral part of the country that I love
For more than 50 years she's ruled this kingdom.
Long may she reign.

Jean M Ellis

The Queen's 80th Birthday

This poem is for our great queen
In memory until the end
Our beautiful and gracious queen
Her next step is around the bend.
A monarch for great England
So beautiful, it isn't true
She steps upon our country land
Whatever happens, England's here
In case you need an extra hand
It is your birthday, give a cheer
I hope you had a lovely day
Thank you also for being great
Happy birthday is what we say
You're eighty now, so hip hooray.

Olivia Sumrie

The Queen

Congratulations on your 80th,
With your smiles and cups of tea.
You make us proud,
You stand your ground.
Long live the Queen!

You keep our traditions,
Representing us so well.
With no privacy at all,
Good, brave and great,
Long live the Queen!

You are so loyal,
You take responsibility seriously.
You make our culture,
You're loved by everyone,
Long live the Queen!

Sophie Greig (12)

The Queen's 80th Birthday Poem

The Queen is simply supreme
For eighty years she has been
She likes to eat scones, jam and cream
Not only has she been seen
As the best Queen there has been
She likes her corgis to be lean!
For as our monarch you see
She must be full of laughter and glee

As for eighty years she has been beautiful and serene
And in many countries still supreme
Her beauty is everlasting seen
And she is our glorious Queen.

Hannah-Louise Callaghan (12)

The River And The Ocean

Bleeding mountains without pain
Carry blessing for your gain
Flowing like lava crick
Passing through a darker cave
Into the heart of unknown.

Secret passion of the earth
Flowing through the holes of hills
Falling into a golden lake
Carry water for a bath
Put out a flame which eats up your vein
Sow it in you barren land
Which is longing, rising sprout.

No more rain for your foiling strain
Flooding rain will wreck your hail
The river nailing a prey
Lets your heart bleed forever.

Put out your passion
In the loin of ocean
Fussy gate will raze your craze.

T Anish

Elizabeth

E ighty today
L ooking so serene
I n a beautiful outfit
Z ippy indeed
A s it's your birthday
B e happy, have fun
E njoy every moment
T he day has just begun
H appy birthday, Your Majesty
   from everyone.

Mavis Gould

Birthday Blessing!

What more can one say
in adulation
For the character and style
that rules our nation?

Her childhood roots
matured before time
because of abdication
and her uncle's decline
to put duty first!
But not Elizabeth!

Like her father before her
and a mother queen divine
Elizabeth, their daughter
remained staunch throughout time!

So *God bless Elizabeth!*
Birthday blessings from above!
is the fervent prayer
of the nation
for our Queen we all love!

Mary Skelton

Happy Birthday Ma'am

Devoted parents gave you grounding
Gave guidance, showing the way
Then came war, sirens sounding
They went and saw
Keeping spirits high
Family matters - order of day

From Princess Elizabeth to majestic Queen
What an eventful reign
Fifty-four years have seen
No cavalier
Willing to comply
Wife, mother, grandma - doubtless acclaim.

Shirley Pinnington

Blest Art Thee

'Twas in April on the twenty-first day,
When the songbird twittered merrily away,

Spreading the news all around,
That you, our Queen, was born safe and sound,

Full of beauty and charmed with love,
Truly sent from Heaven above,

When a child you were so shy,
Especially when in the public eye,

You were the same when in your teens,
Modest and elegant when you were seen,

When you were nearing twenty-one,
A positive young lady you had become,

You show the people that you meet,
There are no strangers in the street,

As they've watched you blossom and grow,
They do love and trust you so,

You always put your people first,
And when your tears are nearing burst,

A brave smile shows upon your face,
Full of pride and charm and grace,

Blest art thee for thy sovereign crown,
Blest art thee for freedom and ground.

Ann Crampton

The First Photograph

I saw the first photograph this very day of our queen,
For nigh on eighty years 'twas hidden away, in a chest, rarely
                                                       to be seen.
A bespectacled gentleman, an eminent photographer cradles
                                             the newborn royal,
I wonder if he knew in that split second of the sacrifice and the toil.

The official version of events show the young princess upon
                                                  a pillow lain,
The radiant Duchess of York smiles sweetly o'er a child destined
                                                      to reign.
That one single moment captured and frozen in time,
Rescued from relative obscurity, stolen away from our eyes,
                                                 such a crime.

The whole world in its entirety looks enviously towards our fair isle,
To have a monarch as loved and respected as ours, oh how we smile.
Of all the rich treasures our planet has been generous to yield,
Her Majesty is most precious, even more than fair meadow or field.

Queen of England, the land of my birth and of my fathers afore,
Queen of the country where I was happily raised 'midst the rich
                                                    and the poor.
Queen of our island both glorious and proud and Queen of
                                                 all our hearts,
And, lest we forget, Queen of the Commonwealth afore
                                               my memory departs.

Michael Hartshorne

A Woman Behind The Crown

To grow as the world looks on
Heads held high with pride and song
A tearful brow with nerves I hide
To grow in stature for a country's pride

A tranquil life your eyes must see
Through palace gates my job is me
Family problems, grief and pride
A mother, a queen with eyes opened wide

To grieve the fallen who gave their life
Queen and country in mind to fight
Through a palace window, just morning mist
Streaming eyes with shaking fist

Not all pampering, jewels and cream
For many years my eyes have seen
Memories of shock, dreams come true
My job as a queen for me and for you.

R S Wayne Hughes

May God Bless The Queen

May God bless the Queen,
We hear everyone shout,
The best there's ever been,
Of that there is no doubt.

We all want to have our say
About the way that we think,
So this very special day
We all have to find a link.

Her birthday is the right time
To show our love once again,
So with this happy rhyme,
We all say, long may she reign!

Gary Jones

The Queen

Congratulations to the Queen,
I hope you had a good birthday.
It's the best one there's ever been,
You rule strongly to this day.

You look over the nation with pride,
Aware of things happening around you.
Not once in your life have you lied
And you are very gentle too.

Sitting down drinking cups of tea,
Walking around with lots of grace.
Reigning over the land gloriously,
Making Britain a better place.

Camille McCrosson (11)

The Queen's 80th Birthday Poem

When thinking of England what comes to mind?
Is it Big Ben or the small country farm?
It is our dear Queen, I think you will find,
Who rules o'er us all with such grace and charm.
Eighty years ago was a different place
But how joyful the year of '26.
You gave such happiness to all your race.
But then came war with bombings and the Blitz.

Your life as princess was every girl's dream,
It was love at first sight with a handsome Greek prince.
Your father's death meant you became our Queen;
We've celebrated your life ever since.

God bless you, Elizabeth, in all that you do;
You're loved by us all, remember that's true!

Dorothy Robertson (12)

Happy Birthday Ma'am

How majestic
Is a reign
Pouring new life
Upon its domain

The sparkles that arise
Comfort those in despair
Time never questions motive
Answers lie well above the grave

Travel clears
The depth of reasons
It brings oil from wells
Veiled or not

My Majesty
From this heart
I speak
Of friendships forged

In unison your subjects
Across this Earth
Bow to your grace
Rejoicing this day

Proud we are
To raise our heads
Our glasses too
Happy birthday Ma'am

Anton Nicholas

Eighty Years

April 1926:

England's future seemed quite forlorn
That dismal year our *Queen* was born.
In April news was very bleak
Wages being cut week on week.
Bitter strikes were being brewed
And cruel actions then ensued.

Caring men in power were few.

Europe's future seemed most forlorn
The very week our *Queen* was born.
There too, life seemed very bleak
Just who will care for poor or weak?
Mussolini, his plans pursues
Though here her birth is joyful news.

Honest men in power were few.

Fast forward now, World War II . . .
That clear young voice, 'I promise you . . .'

April 2006:
May Britain now once more be great
As eighty years *you* celebrate!

Though decent men in power are few.

Dear Ma'am, *your* promises you've kept
And earned our love and great respect.

Anne Everest

The Queen's 80th Birthday

Congratulations on your birthday
You deserve all the pride and cheers
I know you show your love today
Always in every way
You take your duties as they come
To your children you're a super mum
I know you're loyal
And smile all the time
You represent our country
In or out of line
Long live our gracious Queen

Charlotte Emily Tucker (12)

The Queen's Poem

Elizabeth the Second, our reigning queen
Has fifty-four years on the throne been
This year she celebrates being eighty years old
And has, I am sure, many stories to be told.
Dogs, especially corgis, and horses are her passion
But she doesn't care too much for fashion
She is always smart with her matching hat and coat
And is often asked to launch a boat.
Buckingham Palace is where she lives
And Charles, Anne, Andrew and Edward are her four kids
Philip, her husband, is a true gentleman
And he supports the Queen as much as he can.
The Queen attends and supports so many ceremonies
And only wants us to live together in such harmonies.

Lara Cameron (11)

Queen Elizabeth II

Queen Elizabeth was once a princess,
She was then crowned at Westminster Abbey,
At Buckingham Palace is her address,
There is no way it could be shabby.

Her passion for horses is known worldwide,
Whether it be horse racing at Ascot,
Or riding her horse through the countryside,
She also has corgis which she loves a lot.

In sixteen countries she is head of state,
Second longest serving after the King of Thailand,
She's seen ten different prime ministers debate,
And supreme governor of the Church of England.

Windsor was the host of her eightieth birthday,
Long may she reign over us we pray.

Grace Hollingsworth

The Queen's 80th Birthday

After eighty wonderful years
We want to wish you all the best,
As the crowd watches and cheers
We really think you deserve a rest.
Your smile lifts everyone's hearts
Your strength inspires and gives us hope.
When you appear, the clapping starts
With good times and bad you've had to cope.
You always look so smart and neat
With beautiful hats upon your head,
Shiny shoes upon your feet
And corgis waiting to be fed.
But this is what we want to say,
We hope you had a good birthday.

Philippa Batey (12)

Defender Of The Faith

How times have changed since Henry VIII's time;
Five-hundred years of turmoil,
From the fires of Smithfield,
Through the Gunpowder Plot
To the Troubles in Northern Ireland.

Yet, somehow, the Protestant faith has remained intact.
Now, tolerance reigns supreme,
At least, in theory.
We now live in a multi-faith society,
Bringing with it great diversity
Along with conflicting interests,
Real and imagined.

The New Age movement has brought political correctness;
Islam, at its worst, has brought terrorism;
The media feel they are treading on eggshells,
Terrified of offending ethnic minorities.

Yet, through it all,
You have kept the faith
And are not afraid to show it,
Bringing the subject up at Christmas,
Being photographed going to church
When such things are not deemed relevant in today's society.
Few realise just how relevant the Christian faith is,
How important the role, Defender of the Faith,
To a nation uncertain of what it is supposed to believe;
Congratulations, Ma'am, on doing a difficult job.

Kathy Rawstron

Service To The Royal Family

I was born two years before yourself, Your Majesty.
I deem it a privilege to wish you a happy 80th birthday.
I served your father and mother from 1942 until 1945.
Then I served you, Ma'am, from 1956 until 1973.
During this time I first met Your Majesty
When in the guard of honour when you visited Chichester.
This was formed by The Royal Air Force
And Your Majesty paused and spoke to me
To ask where I was in the war
And I explained that I was in battle for the monastery
Where I was shot by a sniper,
I was then medically discharged until 10 years later.
Then I enlisted into The Royal Air Force.
I then became associated with the royal family
As NCO Station Flight in West Raynham, Marham and Goose Bay.
My biggest connection was at Marham
Where I marshalled all the royal flight aircraft from 1970 until 1972
During which time Her Majesty, the Queen Mother
Came in one evening to go to Sandringham to rest with yourself.
When she walked down the steps she reached the last step
And for some reason she stumbled
And I caught her arm to prevent her falling
And when she recovered, she turned and said, 'Thank you, Corporal.'
I carry that with me always.
Happy birthday, Your Majesty and God bless.

Gordon E Miles

Your Majesty

You give to our lives serenity and peace,
Maintaining order in times of great change.
I've watched you standing alone, overseeing your troops,
In one capacity or another.
Always, without exception, you command our respect.
Not with haut or strictness or even expectation.
It simply happens, a natural product, born of loving, caring,
Consideration and, most importantly,
Unconditional acceptance of us all.

The world has witnessed the twists and turns of your family life.
As parents, we share the smiles and the frowns,
Which raising children brings.
In addition to all of this, you played mother to us all.
You stuck with it, you stayed put,
You've remained true to us and to yourself.

'Thank you', Queen Elizabeth, for playing your role in keeping us safe.
'Thank you', God, for giving us this wonderful leader.
And, finally, Your Majesty, 'Happy birthday'.

Janet Scrivens

The Queen 2006

It was April when Easter arrived this year,
The seasons were late and spring not yet here.
To add to our Easter enjoyment,
And lighten the way,
It was the month of Her Majesty's birthday.
A more gracious monarch,
Has never been seen,
And from her loyal subjects,
God save the Queen.

Edward Hill

Born Ter Be Queen

Here in the Black Country,
I'd jus' like ter say,
'appy birthday, yer Majesty,
'ave a gud day.

Eighty a'ter be sniffed at
you've dun ever so well,
an' as a queen, yo' shoud be feelin' quite swell.

Cos when yoh was born,
no one cud a known,
that in '53, you'd be Queen on a throne.

But you've dun yer best,
an' I'm 'appy ter say,
mid all ups an' downs,
yoh dun it yohr way.

An' a ruddy gud job yoh med on it, an all.
Carry on the gud werk.

God bless our Queen.

Jacqueline Claire Davies

Happy Birthday

Congratulations on your special day,
The love of your people
Say have a happy, happy birthday!
I hope you get some lovely presents,
That bring you joy and fun,
We're glad you are our Queen,
You are the best, the very best,
Three cheers say everyone,
God save the Queen!

Emily Culpeper (11)

The Heart Of Being Her Majesty

Grand dreams and royal liaisons,
A mayflower, once despised, yet pressed to bloom,
The royal bloodline tied up in many nations.
The birthright of a future Majesty, nursing softly within her womb.

Set in days of boredom,
Her heart a protective shield,
The heritage of deportment, and decorum.
Unbending and demanding, slowly gives its yield.

The changing of set horizons,
Darkening clouds that roll,
Yet happy is the bride the sun does shine on.
Despite its emotional toll.

A regal poise that won over a smitten nation,
Upon your head, a glittering crown,
A queen magnificently arrayed, in a modern age foundation.
By heritage, separated, too your subjects dedicated,
Yet, stands isolated, and alone.

Seldom do you wear depression,
And tears when hurt, you ne'er let display,
Your heart toils its heavy burden, and the showering of affection,
Is grasped by all, even on this, your special day.

And I think we are privileged in a very special sort of way,
For the survival of the monarchy (to choruses of disapprobation),
Guided by the hand of providence, spanning generations,
Even beyond this present lay,
Was the heart of being Her Majesty,
And was in itself its great salvation.
Happy birthday, Queen Elizabeth,
From every heart and tongue that graces life upon God's creation,
Upon this, your very special day.

Glenwyn Peter Evans

To Your Majesty Queen Elizabeth

Ma'am, may I wish you every happiness
Upon this great day, of blessedness
Upon your special eightieth official birthday
With lots of special events, that will be on display

As the blackbirds greet you, with notes of cheers
With notes of alarm, as the sun appears
As the mistle thrush listens, upon a tree
But soon to join in, with the blackbirds' notes so free

Such joyful notes, sounds just like a praise
Surely, greeting Your Majesty, with their notes of phrase
Such a contrast, as church bells chime, so merrily
Oh, what a blessing, whilst, listen in, to the melody

Such pleasure, to watch the changing of the guards
Giving so much joy, with splendid regards
Just for this great day, for the nation to see
Especially, for your gracious and lovely Majesty

What a wonderful day, a beautiful scenery
To rejoice, that God has made for you, through His victory
The gaiety, carnivals, the golden coach, and beautiful horses
To catch our hearts, through these very good courses

Magical, enchanting, gracefully dancing, as the night shadows fall
Whilst dancing till midnight, till the early morn does call
So, as I wish you every happiness, Your Majesty,
                                        through years to come
Reign, as long as the great God permits, till, maybe day is done

Jean McGovern

To The Queen

You are sweet, kind and loyal,
I love you with all my heart
And, what's more, you are royal
And you really play your part.
Your birthday will soon be here,
Celebration time and cheer
That is very, very near
At this special time of year.
You are very glorious,
Happy, pretty and willing
And very victorious,
You make our life fulfilling,
So really enjoy your day
In a special kind of way.

Daniella Humble (11)

The Queen

Congratulations from 18 to 80
You made it all this way
You stand up for Great Britain
And I'm glad to hear you say
'My husband and I are glad to be
Amongst this happy crowd
And hear all the children sing
The anthem very loud.'

You help the country and keep it healthy
You also keep us happy.
You try your very best
To never ever get snappy.
You're pretty, delightful
And carry a smile.
Long live the Queen.

Katherine Mundy (11)

Her Majesty!

She leads our country with wisdom
Reflecting her senior years
She has experienced her own share of life
Including troubled times and tears

We are blessed with her love and devotion
As leader of our fair land
With the love of her family
And Prince Philip at her right hand

We thank the Lord for her guidance
And are comforted as the future is unclear
As we celebrate the occasion of her 80th year

Kevin Clark

A Poem For The Queen

Her Majesty the Queen is 80 now,
She travels the world in a royal plane,
She remembers all of her marriage vows
And thinks about her husband again and again.

Her Majesty has had some glorious years,
She has made some royal peers,
To guide the UK in the right way,
She owns the mint which gives out pay.

Elizabeth loves her family and her corgis,
And looks over everyone with praise,
She has quite a few years' occasions,
The British public like to raise.

So Your Majesty this poem is just for you,
To celebrate 80 years of your joy,
So may your reign last forever
And your kindness brings happiness to every girl and boy.

Matthew Willbye

The Nation's Mother

A fine lady, she rides on her horse
A true leader of our nation
Responsible, generous and dignified
To her people gives inspiration

She has lived through the Second World War
The fall of the Soviet Union, how it would be
And two wars fought in Iraq
And the death of John F Kennedy

She endured the abdication of her uncle
The dramatic death of Princess Di did appal
The endless ups and downs and relationship
With her daughter-in-law, The Duchess of Cornwall

Elizabeth II, we honour and respect you
Great love from our hearts is hurled
To you, a grandmother, aunt and cousin
Britain remains the envy of the world

You are doing a truly wonderful job
May you reign for many more years
No greater role model for our children and ourselves
The nation's mother whom we greatly revere

C M Armstrong

Hail The Queen

Hail our Queen for she's eighty today
and we shall celebrate with her this way.
She's been a shining star for all to see
and a role model that we want to be.

Happy birthday, our dear old Queen
you are still radiant as though you are a teen
As we celebrate with you today, when you clock eighty
we pray you live long to be ninety.

Ojuola Tolulope

Hail The Queen

Lady Elizabeth
Queen of going days
My priceless jewel
In radiance of beauty
Brightening the British crown
On the throne of England.

Though a distance away
I hold the unperished admiration
With an undiminished desire
Sailing on waters of Nigeria
In the breathing spot of Calabar.

To pull my peers to your sphere
As raising queens of Africa
That there be love in our lands
Against the ills of AIDS
As above the punch of poverty
For wholesome days
That await our children
As daughters of Buckingham Palace.

Evelyn Oti

A Birthday Wish

Happy birthday dear Queen Elizabeth, happy birthday to you,
I am sending my best wishes with the smell of a fresh rose too.
I hope you have a sunny day filled with very big surprises,
showered with love and affection from morn till night-time passes.

A cake with flickering candles, how beautiful that will be.
Smiling, smiling all day long like a rainbow's beam.
A birthday is very special like seeing angels fly, have a wonderful
birthday our Queen Elizabeth, shed no tears but dry.

Dear Queen of England, I will say a prayer for you, magical
moments, magical moments, I hope on this day will unfold, like all the
fairies gathering in the fields of gold.

Madeline Reade

My Inspiration

Oh lady of serene goodwill
Who upholds our British life
Honest and loyal to all Christian faith
An example, as daughter, mother, wife
For few would want to tread the path
That you have trod throughout your reign
Bound to bow to government rules
With no reward and little gain
We have watched you age to eighty
Seen your patience and your smile
Your love for family, dogs and horses
And your dignity all the while
But Britain never should forget
The important part that history plays
And you are part of that great scene
To serve and love for all your days.

June Davies

In True Celebration

To a gracious and dedicated lady, our beloved Queen
Upright to truth and faith you have always been seen
A royal face hiding from the world her personal sorrows
Yet giving us that reassurance for our brighter tomorrows
To millions of your subjects, Your Majesty stands paramount
Loved from princess to sovereign, far more than we can count
You're still the Queen of everyone's heart and so it remains
Fixed in the history books as the House of Windsor proclaims.

May we celebrate this, your eightieth birthday, Ma'am.

Dawn Prestwich

Happy Birthday, Ma'am

Elizabeth, Alexandra, Mary
Lillibet, Your Majesty, our Queen
You were born, Ma'am, to a hard task:
To be sovereign over our land.
Thrust as a young mother, into office,
At the untimely death of your dad.

You looked vulnerable, yet regal,
In the pomp of your coronation.
You carried yourself with dignity and honour,
We admired your tenacity and selflessness.

Your attention to detail, adherence to duty,
Ma'am, you have served us well.
Your serene smile has heartened us
Through much trial and tribulation,
You never shirked from serving us,
Even in your 'annus horribilis'.

We celebrate with you now, Ma'am,
On this, your eightieth birthday
And wish you many, many more,
Long may you reign over us!

Ann Sutcliffe

Old Age Speckles

Having inhaled the youthful years up
old age speckles appear, one after another
like dusk
like the soaks of an old wall.

Old age speckles, the footmarks
of the time, muttering to itself
many past things and intelligence cemented
with happiness, blood and tears . . .

Hsu Chi Cheng

A Poem For The Queen

As one who's keen to praise our Queen, now in her eightieth year,
I here defend and recommend, the rule all should revere:
Loyalty to royalty must be the golden rule,
It's loyalty to royalty that makes Britannia cool.
If Boadicea tried to be a queen who ruled with might
Why run her down? She earned her crown by winning many a fight!
Most rulers own that on the throne, they're prone to make mistakes,
Which tells us why or so say I, King Alfred burnt the cakes.
If King Canute was not astute, we shouldn't be dismayed,
At least he tried to stem a tide, which sadly disobeyed.
Though Harold's reign went down the drain beside the Sussex shore,
He did his best to win the quest, as good kings will at war.
Who cares one jot if John was not a good man all the time?
Quite often kings get up to things, it isn't such a crime.
Why criticise those small white lies that fell from Henry's lips
When ways and means of winning queens were at his fingertips?
Who thinks the less of Good Queen Bess for using powers of state
To ship all those she deemed as foes, along to Traitors' Gate?
In wisdom schooled, our monarchs ruled and ruled the royal way
With all the pace and charm and grace shown by our Queen today.
So when men scorn the highly born, remember this, my friend:
It's loyalty to royalty that matters in the end!
This sceptred isle has cause to smile and so let none abstain
But with me raise a glass to praise our Queen - long may she reign!

Alan Millard

Majesty

King Edward's crown upon her head, a much
different life to the one she had led.
A crowning moment which was for life, and
a prince who pledged his life to his Queen and wife.

Majesty

Watched by millions across the world, what kind
of thoughts that, in their heads, whirled.
For a daunting prospect, before them unfurled,
with a task before them, for as yet untold.

Majesty

They rose to the occasion as they were want
neither had said don't or can't.
For the monumental task ahead, oh how
they must have had aching necks.

Majesty

May you always reign, steadfast and true
with your love beside you, who is true blue, and
stand for *right* and *might* and *truth*.
Whoever trespass, the day may rue
for Q*ueen* and *country* we'll never lose.

Majesty.

Rosemary Peach

The Corgi Story

I saw a corgi outside the shops,
When I was young, and thought of the Queen.
Sniffing at discarded lollipops,
His toffee fur, squeaky-clean, pristine.

I thought someone had stolen her dog!
I thought the Queen *only* had corgis!
As the neglected pooch, eyed up mogs,
I gave in to the urge, set him free!

'Head back to the palace!' I screamed aloud,
The dog's tongue just lolled dumb in the sun.
He just sat there, puffed out his chest proud.
People passed by, papers pumped with puns.

The corgi wouldn't leave the shop door,
Even with his lead unclasped and free!
A girl came out, he held up his paw:
Phew! The Queen's with her, drinking tea.

Sarah Louise Parry

A Birthday Greeting For Her Majesty The Queen

I well remember how sincere
You were in what you said
And how you promised that you'd serve,
And so you have.

For us the years have sped.
And through the many changes
You've truly kept your word.

So happy birthday!
Receive our thanks;
You have upheld your most exacting role
Just as you said.

Peter Spurgin

God Bless Her Majesty

Born in 1926 and from the year 1936, Elizabeth has been Princess,
Heir Presumptive and Queen Elizabeth II.

Her long line of ancestors have given us one of the most
historical lines in the world.

Like her father and grandfather before her, Elizabeth has served
her country and Commonwealth, in good times and difficult times.

In sickness and in health. in peacetime and in war,
she has been with us to lead and to guide.

The Queen's loyal husband, Prince Philip, Duke of Edinburgh,
her mother, sister and the royal children have supported her.

As with all people, the Queen has had good times
and heartbreaking times.

But at the end of the day, her leadership has been of the most
wonderful ever known.

Let us salute Her Majesty in this, her 80th year.
May God bless her and be with her now and for evermore.

Janet Cavill

Easter Royal

A happy celebration is in hand,
For the royal lady of our land.
A happy birthday to our Queen,
Her 80th birthday, what a dream.

A busy lady there is no doubt,
As she does her duty and walkabout
She will know the true meaning of Easter Day,
Spending the morning at church to pray.

So all good wishes on her day,
With family and friends around her to stay.
She is widely thought of near and far,
So wish her well wherever you are.

Evelyn M Harding

Our Queen

I am just a little older than our dearly loved and gracious Queen,
But I'm sure recalling memories of events which we have seen,
Must be of similar qualities, both proud and oft-times sad
As we remember wartime serving in ATS uniform clad.
I wore with pride my khaki dress and felt important too
Knowing our then renowned princess was in our army too.
The sadness came when King George died, unhappiness for all,
And I was also in Kenya where our princess heard the monumental call
To take on the mantle of the greatest job of all,
To become our monarch, though so young, she faced it with
                                                great fortitude
And with her husband by her side this courage has continued,
Through difficulties in our land and in her family too.
She has been an inspiration, a guide for me and you
To handle life's adversities with Her Majesty's grace and care,
In England we are so well blessed, here more than anywhere.

Many mental images are printed on the mind,
The Mall, great coaches, flags aloft and cheers from all combined,
To create an atmosphere of joy and much affection
Riding her horse by side-saddle, with dignified perfection,
To join the scene on Horse Guards to greet the soldiers smart
For the Trooping the Colour day, in which she plays a part,
A beautiful picture in her tunic of bright red,
A great sight to remember, it has to be said.
This special day, by no means all,
Countless others we could recall
But long may she reign from her 80th celebration
And I'm sure I speak with heart and soul from all corners of the nation
In wishing her peace, good health and happiness untold,
Shared with Prince Philip, these qualities of gold.

Happy birthday and God bless you, Ma'am.

E B Soltys

The Queen - Your 80th Birthday

It is this country's happy fate
To have a much loved Head of State.
Salute her Majesty the Queen.
For many years her reign has been
A service to the Commonwealth,
A service to this country's health;
Above the politics and strife
To raise the quality of life.

It was a most traumatic thing
To lose our brave, courageous king.
The tragedy was not foreseen;
The young princess became our Queen.
Your tears and fears, they were not shown,
With dignity you graced the throne.

Your charming smile
And twinkling eyes,
Scatter the dark clouds
From the skies.

Throughout the years our love has grown
Towards the Queen we call our own.
God bless our Queen is what we pray;
May you remain for many a day.

Queen of the United Kingdom,
Sovereign of the Commonwealth,
May we take this liberty
And wish you happiness and health.

(This tribute may be late, I fear,
Nevertheless, it is sincere).

John Freeth

A Real Princess

How long had I stood shivering in cotton dress,
now getting wet as rain began to fall.
I felt a right drip, standing so still,
with all my mates, along Tulse Hill.
Soon the open-topped car came into view.

It was you, Ma'am, you waved as your car
drove slowly by.
'A real princess,' I said, with tears of joy
in my eyes.

Suddenly I called out your name, you turned
and gave me a radiant smile,
I felt really proud to have waited so long,
waved my flag and cheered extra loud.
Even if, by now, I was soaking wet,
right down to my thermal vest.

Maureen Connolly (nee Creissen)

Coral Waves

All England fills the merry street
As come about the British Fleet,
Hard wrought in Nelson's seas and wiles.

Do nought but compliment her smiles,
Great banners hoisted gleefully
For Lillibet in Jubilee,
In sea of red and white and blue,
A waterfall of bannered Mall.

'God save our gracious Queen,' they call,
Royal Guard and Air Force, brave her crew,
So many, so much owe 'so few'.

Yet, all that clamour, this, her day,
Cannot such glamour stow away,
Shall not her coral costume best,

More beautiful . . . than all the rest.

Roger Mosedale

A Letter To Her Majesty Upon Her 80th Birthday

Might it not remain a dream
That one day I shall come to London
To visit the Queen.

Not because I'm a stranger
But by the wisdom you humbly asked
That Your Majesty might lend an open ear.

Here, all ears have been buried
In Prejudgement's parched ground.
Of Understanding's men and women,
                            none could be found.

Was it something I shouldn't have said?
What have I done to merit such disbelief
Even from hearts whose beats I trusted as a child?

Beneath Jesus' Cross stood Mary and John.
The Devil has his demons.
I . . . What have I? Nothing!

Save for the myth of God and His favour,
Which I created, not without grave reason.
I might yet, here, be condemned for treason.

As a true believer of freedom and dignity as
Birthright of all of humanity, I am your subject,
As one who might at last see Jesus in me -

You are the spiritual mother I've never had.
Before you, then, with head bowed and eyelids lowered,
My back to your silent subjects,

I shall make yet one last plea:
That there in the land that bears your people's
Standard and good name,

Find me guilty
And lock me up forever
Or set me free.

Jonel Abellanosa

The Queen - Her Way

Abdication of their uncle
Robbed two young sisters
Of their private family lives
Elizabeth was protective.

They joined the Girl Guides together
When the family moved to Windsor
After war broke out.
Camping in Windsor Great Park
And had happy times,
Despite the darkening days ahead
Learned to get along with people.

A love of dogs and horses
Started at an early age and never took less importance,
As the years went by she enjoyed the outdoors.

Growing up in the shadow of danger,
And determined to do her bit.

Joined up and driving a car,
Learning to be a mechanic
Was her way of helping the war effort.

Victory and peace,
Marriage and a family grown.
Difficult times and happy times shared
Time has flown, passed like planes over the palace.

Now grandchildren occupy her thoughts,
Dogs and horses too have their special place.
What you loved as a girl is part of the heart of life.

Freda Grieve

Dear Ma'am

It's me - it's me - an admirer true
Penning this message especially for you
I'm a humble fool who is known as 'John'
Like you - regretting so many years have, alas, gone
Eighty years since we two were born
Into a land by a national strike torn
You've shown your worth in many ways
Born before me by just six days
Although, of course, your coming was blessed
Before I was born at least six nappies you had messed
Brought down to Earth too suddenly
To become one no longer free
Enjoying a break then happily
When your father was taken away from thee
This world has changed - our hair colour too
But nothing grey could be said about you
We are so grateful that you are our Queen
To have you near, a joy supreme
Girls dream of being princesses one day
But never the Queen with her freedom taken away
You have that smile that lifts each heart
We all wish that you will never from us, part
Enjoy this time, it is all yours
Accept our love and too applause
May you never ever leave our 'family'
A very happy birthday - Your Majesty.

John L Wright

Queen Elizabeth II 80th Birthday

A happy 80th birthday, Your Majesty,
All good wishes go to you from me.
An eventful life you have had.
You became our Queen with the demise of your dad.

Successive governments you have seen,
We all rely on you, our Queen.
Over 50 years you have reigned,
Much esteem you have gained.

Always regal and sincere,
Champion the things you hold dear.
Never lost your equilibrium,
Always a lady, always a mum.

You've had your share of sorrows,
Right is yours in all our tomorrows.
Long may you reign over us,
As is your right, without favour or fuss.

God bless you in your 80th year,
May you have everything you hold dear.

Olive Young

A Special Birthday

Many years, some with tears
Have passed before your eyes.
Love sublime, has filled your time
With greetings and goodbyes.
Fond memories, public ceremonies
While all have played a part,
Genteel smiles, across the miles
Have softened many hearts.
So embrace, today with grace
And let the bells toll loud,
Now eighty years, yes, but we all guess
You must be feeling proud.

Maureen Steele

A Royal Celebration

C ome one, come all
O ne's voice to raise
N ow is the time
G reetings are sent
R egal words, ascent
A cross the country
T he public agree
U nanimously
L oud cheers they give
A nd all for thee
T heir honour
I s for Her Majesty
O ne's birthday to toast
N ow, hip hooray
S overeign, our Queen we praise.
       Ma'am

Peter G H Payne

The Power And The Blood

The Queen's colours are red and gold - blood and power.
One represents war and death, the other strength and wealth.
The Queen is military - shooting, tanks and guns.
It's written on a café wall at Harewood House.
The Queen is strong, labours hard and has the ability to
                                            overcome suffering
Ten extra years over three score years and ten, making eighty in all.
The Queen is death and rebirth, something special at Easter time.
She is the light, she is the resurrection.
She is death, she is wealth.
The power of the land.
Compromise it and the nation weakens.
Take it away, the nation falls.
From the little man to the big, big man, all say -
        'God save the Queen, she is the power, give her the Earth
                                            for it is fading away'.

Philip Loudon

Celebration

Your Majesty, I wish for you
In this, your 80th year
A future of good fortune
Of happiness, joy and cheer.

A future blessed with inward strength
Which comes from one on high,
A strength that conquers every fear
That comes as time goes by.

In this year of celebration
May you find peace afresh
Remembering happy memories
With those you've loved the best.

May you have many happy years
To reign as our dear Queen,
With much love from all your family
To enhance your royal scene.

M S Bradley

Eightieth Birthday

Throughout the world she's held in high esteem -
Admired as the Queen who reigns supreme.
For more than fifty years our faithful Ma'am
Has ruled consistently with pride and charm
And trodden paths no monarch trod before
Earning devotion on each foreign shore.
With royal duties, tirelessly performed,
The hearts of this whole nation have been warmed.

The dignity and grace that she displays
Are worthy of our love, respect and praise.
So let us form this nation's longest queue
Expressing heartfelt thanks, (long overdue)
And raise a glass the good old British way
To wish our much-loved Queen - *Happy Birthday!*

Joy Saunders

Untitled

To yourself you have to keep, my lady of England can't you see.
You have set our country free. I applaud your stubbornness,
If I may say.
I hope that I do not offend in any way.
Such a strong lady, oh you are.
A commoner I am, but just so proud of my country.
Frightened to lose you, oh Your Majesty
No one could have beaten the tragedy you have had,
I am so sorry,
I will fight for our country too.
I wish it was the way it was when your husband and yourself
Could bear that cross, of love.
You are a family, as it should be, dear Queen of ours.
I have three. Two little children and a wonderful husband,
May I add you cannot count it on two hands.
The time we've been together is 18 years - what bliss.
No more tears,
My two little babies. Third one, my hubby.
I am so proud of my country and proud of England.

Wendy Deaves

To Our Queen - A Happy Birthday

I'd sat all night on the Mall-side grass,
Waiting, dear Ma'am, to see you pass,
There, on your coronation day
Centre of all its royal display.
As you came back crowned, you turned your head
Smiling and joyous, and I said,
'Oh you pretty dear, you pretty dear!'
A loving cry that you couldn't hear.
So many years on - we love you still,
Our gracious Queen by God's goodwill.
May this, your 80th birthday, be
As happy, Ma'am, and from sorrows free.

Kathleen M Hatton

Here's To Elizabeth

So gallant a girl, not long a bride,
Stricken with grief for the father who'd died.
Stepped down from a plane one sad noontide
To take up the reins of her duty.

Not for her now, any private life;
Limited times to be mother and wife.
It's the public pageantry, drum and fife,
That mark out the terms of her duty.

Solemn her vows as her head was crowned.
A lifetime of service, before God, she owned.
And her people's rejoicing - a tumultuous sound -
Welcomed the start of her duty.

A lifetime of service none could deny,
As the years have fled and the world's gone awry.
Now the media harass and tabloids stand by
Hoping she'll fail in her duty.

Greedy, her people, with envious eyes
Complain about privilege but can't surmise
The weight of the burden. Still, they'd criticise
If she took a break from her duty.

So gallant a lady! At eighty she still
Toils in our service and works with a will.
When we'd have retired long since she'll fulfil
The relentless requirements of duty.

So here's to Elizabeth! Long may she reign!
We are grateful for freedoms she's helped to sustain
And we'll shout hurrah, again and again
As we watch her performing her duty.

Anne Wild

The Queen Of England

A tribute to Your Highness at eighty years
Where your eyes have seen more than most
Whilst sitting from your throne in a family life
We give thanks and raise our glass to your toast.

The years have been kind to your smiling heart
Your presence as the Queen has played the part
So auspiciously toward the community large
In a world much bigger than England's barge.

You remain scented and Head of State
As an orchid's glory pure to delight
The honour to have you is with loyalty
For you are the one whose face is royalty.

You have seen us through the dregs of mayhem
With wisdom reveared by your hindsight
When the talebearer has borne us indignity
By the infringements of war and poverty.

We honour your grace, your love and zest
For you are the Queen of England's best
Your place has timely been with us all
So accept this gesture for your anniversary ball.

PS: Happy birthday to Queen Elizabeth
　　Your most esteemed and Highness Royal
　　May your celebration be a United Kingdom
　　Filled with joyous cheer from England's toil.

PPS:　Shame about the World Cup 2006
　　　And Beckham on International
　　　Television saying 'F**k as if
　　　In Four Weddings and a Funeral.
　　　C'est la vie, 'Viva Italia'.

Anthony Rosato

Gratitude

Deep within a marbled palace and upon a golden throne,
There's a lady sitting motionless, as if she were of stone,
She's a servant of the people, yet we still refuse to see
That her goldfish bowl existence is a thrall in luxury.

We require she lead the charges when the nation's out in force,
And make act of great contrition when the plans get blown off course,
We demand that she step forward when we need to treat with foes,
Be a diplomat exemplar whose opinion never shows.

We insist she's first at kneeling when we fear it's time to pray,
And then on to lead the cheering when we say it's time to play,
It's her job to keep her finger on the pulse of how we feel,
It's a labour such that Hercules might baulk at the ordeal.

Though deferred to with all honour, ultimately she's the slave,
Of a people who instruct her as to how she must behave,
She can never make an error, fearing ill-informed attack,
And accept in her position, she can never answer back.

She has borne our stately burden now for over fifty years,
And accepted all the brickbats, all the jeering and the sneers,
We have taken it for granted that she'll never go away
Yet we rarely stop to thank her, well God bless you, Ma'am, I say.

James Melrose

Queen's 80th Birthday

Plans are in place
To pay homage to the Queen
Here's hoping the celebrations
Will be the best she's ever seen
Although her official birthday
Is the 17th of June
Her actual one is in April
And will be with us very soon

Reaching eighty is a milestone
Hope life does the same for me
She's very fit and active
As everyone can see
She carries out her duties
Visiting countries far away
Always a smile on her face
Whatever the time of day

Over and throughout her eighty years
She's had her tales of woe
Just like any family
What a way to go
She's always held her head high
No matter what's gone on
Let's hope Charles can do the same
Proving he is his mother's son.

Martha Ann D'Souza

The Queen

Queen Elizabeth, pride of England
Admire her for many, many reasons
The grace, the dignity and charm
Decency, command and splendour
Palaces and many servants aside
She retains humility and respect
Along with even bits of solitude
Life sure has had its ups and downs
And why should she be an exception
The perseverance she has shown
Belongs only and only to her alone
And yet she smiles in a very special way
Years back when I was a schoolboy
She came to town for a state visit
And drove by, in a special motorcade
We wore turbans and waved our hands
But could not see inside the motorcade
That didn't bother us, as she was there
That is all that mattered then
It still does now.

Aijaz Gul

The Queen Of Hearts

You gleam like a diamond on your throne,
Fiery like a flame in your eighth decade,
Oh Majesty, you give England your amber light.

Under your golden shadow, the nation lies,
Protected by your arsenals, England glows,
And you may, forever, live,
God save you, Your Majesty.

Tri Tran

Happy Easter And Happy Birthday Greetings

Happy Easter and happy birthday.
An opportunity to convey
our very best wishes, Ma'am, to you
on your eightieth birthday too.

We knew, like you, those long war years.
Witnessed heartache and so many tears.
Then we saw our country stand with pride.
Such sadness now as standards slide . . .

We mourn too, the loss of give and take.
See so many greedy on the make.
but there are still good folk, honest and true
and we send heartfelt greetings to you.

Valerie Ovais

Elizabeth Regina

Elizabeth, Queen of Great Britain
You have us totally smitten!
Lady of immeasurable charm,
Your smile is genuine and warm.

You personify grace and majesty
Being blessed with a delicate beauty
You set an impeccable example as Queen
Never has your equal been!

During times of war you shone like a beacon of light
And brought hope into the darkness of night.
You served your country with rare dedication
We're proud to call you Queen of our nation!

On this, your 80th birthday
Allow us to say 'Viva, la Reine!'
Honour us with your smile, again and again.

Iris Ina Glatz

To Be A Head Of A Nation

Caged in a golden carriage,
Paraded in front of its admirers,
Its wings cropped
Not allowed to be one with the wind.
Duty comes first,
Serving destiny.
There is no sun for the caged bird.

Shadows of knights
Guard their queen.
Only in her sleep is she free.
In her rose garden
A galloping horse rides the wind.
The moon is her consolation,
The silver mirror of the sun.

The golden cage still sparkles in the sun,
The faithful see her crown as bright as light.
The citizens of a great nation, hear her silent song,
A song of love, a disciplined love.
A love that builds your nation,
The foundation of a good home is still love.
The Queen of a great nation, Elizabeth II.

Yoko Hand

Birthday Greetings To Elizabeth R

Our Queen has reached her 80th year,
She has ruled us strong and shown no fear,
A shy young girl of twenty-one
She kept her promise and took the Monarchy on
To wear the crown and be Head of State.
So dignified and calm, right up to date.
An institution she would never forsake.
So, from your subjects, our greetings
Are now full of joy.
Happy birthday, Your Majesty
And we hope you may have many many more!

Jean Dutfield

Regal Respect

I was taught to stand to attention when the National Anthem played,
hands by my sides, proudly singing -
a respect for my Queen displayed.

I made scrapbooks of the royal family,
played with my coronation coach with golden doors and horses.

I have a sense of pride. Although you are a queen,
your son helped my son through his Prince's Trust.
I think of both our sons with affection.
I stand quietly in reflection.

During the coronation with all the crowds so dense,
I was too young to represent my school.
I just sat on my garden fence.
The special train passed by, so grand -
I waved my flags - she waved her hand!
How cool!

Then came the Jubilee,
Her Majesty waved to my children,
so close in the narrow street -
out to the harbour we followed.

'Hello again!' she called, 'I've seen you before!'
Happy birthday, Queen Elizabeth,
from me, your loyal friend.

I don't want presidents ruling these isles,
I'll support *you* to the end.

J W Whiteacre

Happy Birthday, Your Majesty

Happy birthday, Your Majesty
Now you are eighty years old
But still you carry that sparkle
A smile of pure silver and gold

You have had your ups and downs
You have seen so many things
You have wined and dined dignitaries
The ordinary to queens and kings

You have travelled so many miles
Giving pleasure to all you meet
Seeing all those smiling faces
As you wave and finally greet

Animals play a big part in your life
A part of your life and leisure
Being involved with them all
Must give to you great pleasure

A mother and the Head of State
Sometimes must have been a strain
You have always had the strength
That has shown throughout your reign

We wish you all the very best
For all the years you've been
We are very grateful for the pleasure
You have given for being our Queen

Malcolm G Bradshaw

Our Modern Monarch

Queen Elizabeth the Second, is eighty this year,
the first child of a duke and duchess.
It was not her destiny to become a queen,
but she certainly has been a success.
In 1947, she married her prince
nearly sixty years ago.
In 1952, she ascended the throne;
so his career, then had to go.

Elizabeth, a wife and mother
whose family are her life.
But like every other mother,
she has had trouble and strife.
Head of State and Commonwealth
she travels around the globe,
to meet and greet her subjects,
she certainly enjoys the job.

She has four grown-up children
including a son and heir.
But while she is fit and able,
she intends to stay right there.
The Queen is a wonderful person,
and is a great sovereign -
so 'Happy birthday, Your Majesty,
and long may you reign'.

Doreen E Hampshire

Easter Birthday

Here's wishing you a happy 80th Easter birthday, Ma'am.
I know how it feels to be 80!
I'm 82 but my life would be strange to you.
Your life would be impossible for me.
How you can, at your time of life, live it constantly in the public eye,
It would be anathema to me, I need my privacy!
For in this time I live my life in art and poetry,
For at the age of eighty odd, there is far too much reality -
While the inner visions make life more bearable for me,
You, as the Queen of England and the Commonwealth,
Have been a source of inspiration to so many.
You too have borne and weathered
The many storms and stresses of your life,
Your high ideals have enabled you to do so.
Based deep in Christianity, the message of the Risen Lord at Easter
Has meaning for you too,
Long may you continue -
God bless and keep you.
Long life and happiness
Queen Elizabeth Secundo.

Patricia Arnett

Our Queen

Graceful and tactful, that is our Queen.
Gentle and caring, the head of the team.
This year she's eighty, I hope she'll have fun,
With cream cake and sherry, cos she's number one.

M Wilcox

A Tribute

As antelope passed by the lodge,
They maybe sensed the scene.
A king had died and by Man's laws,
A princess was now our Queen.

And so began in Africa,
This Elizabethan age.
How would our new and fledgling Queen,
Cope with the centre stage?

Her willingness to adapt to change,
Was shown some years before.
She trained to drive large army trucks,
For a nation then at war.

And so throughout the many years,
She's been our Head of State.
Our way of life has altered much
And all at quite a rate.

But true to form she's kept her head,
Midst problems numbering plenty.
It seems when pressed to make reforms,
She cries, 'Festina lente!'

Despite the growing global threat,
To culture and tradition,
The influence of our Sovereign Head,
Has helped thwart opposition.

You've ruled with dedication, Ma'am,
Preserved what you hold dear.
We wish you health and happiness,
In this, your eightieth year!

David Anderson

Her Majesty's Birthday

God save the Queen, Elizabeth or Lillibet.
She is eighty years old and gracious yet.
And, like her subjects, has her ups and downs.
Tries to meet it all without a frown.

The press always try to catch her smiles.
For her frowns, also, they travel miles.
With dignity and poise, she is well trained.
The love of her subjects she has gained.

She is a mother with three boys and a girl.
They have had their problems and left her in a whirl.
Elizabeth the Second lost her sister and mother,
Another princess was killed. A scandal like no other.

A modern queen in a modern world,
The Union Jack we will keep unfurled
To pay our respects in our own way.
Wish her a long life and a happy birthday!

Ellen Spiring

Queen Elizabeth's 80th Birthday

Happy birthday wishes, dear, Queen Elizabeth so great and noble
You have long reigned over us with fortitude, happy and glorious
May happiness and peace be with you all your days, in so many ways
God bless you, dear Queen, and all your beloved family too,
Happy birthday to you!

Janet Wright

Tribute To Her Majesty
(On the occasion of her 80th Birthday)

Adored by all the people from a very tender age
We collected snapshots of you, gleaned from printed page
Then later on a calendar with sister, Margaret Rose
Featured curly-topped princesses in a childhood pose
The almanac outdated, but still as I recall
For years that pretty picture had pride of place on wall

Brownies, Girl Guides, growing up, then sadly came a war
You donned yet another uniform, which, with pride, you wore
Your wedding day finally arrived, and we observed with pride
A lovely regal lady with her prince close by her side
We shared your grief at later date, for we were grieving too
But a lion's cub, born to be Queen, did what she had to do

Motherhood soon followed, in this we shared your joy
So anxiously awaited your firstborn baby boy
Other children followed to enhance your family
Now we wonder where the years went, mums like you and me
We've revelled in the happiness and fought the sprinkled tears
Of changing times, but still come smiling through the years

Please accept this as a tribute to your dedicated life
We know it's not been easy being sovereign, mum and wife
So may we wish you happiness and pray the coming years
Bring you deserved contentment, free from troubled cares
On the occasion of your birthday, Ma'am, may we drink a toast
God bless Queen Elizabeth, our beloved royal host.

Bell Ferris

The Queen

She has lived a good life
Has been a good queen
And now, in her 80th year
Reigns supreme
There have been
Many changes
Throughout all her life
She has travelled the world
Shared in each country's plight
Has a presence and grace
Wherever she goes
Has a worldwide respect
As everyone knows
We wish her a day of enjoyment
And cheer
Our Queen, as she reaches
Her 80th birthday this year

Jeanette Gaffney

The Queen Is Eighty

Eighty years since, a princess was born
She arrived into the world, on a summer's morn
And as a girl, it wasn't expected to be seen
That this young princess would become our Queen.

She served in the ATS during the war
And helped to keep the enemy from our shore
After the death of her father, it was to be seen
That this young princess was our future Queen.

Then she got married to Prince Philip and what's more
To the Royal Family, she added, her children of four
So eighty years on, our wish for today
Your Majesty, have a 'Happy 80th Birthday'.

Colin Metcalfe

One And All

'Happy Birthday', Ma'am, to you
on this, your 80th year.
No doubt blessing all you have
and those that you hold dear . . .

'Happy Birthday' to all those
who also follow suit.
No doubt counting what you need
to budget on your loot . . .

People the world over,
rich and poor - unblest,
all dream of understanding
the plight of all the rest . . .

So happy birthday one and all,
if only dreams came true,
everyone would be in line
for health and happiness to accrue . . .

Melody

Here's A Health Unto Your Majesty

How happy the news on that April day
Those eighty years ago,
A princess born! but whose future lay
As monarch this realm to know.
Steadfast to her dedication,
Gracious in all dealings.
Strength when troubles test the nation.
Joy when bells are pealing.
Happy birthday - Your Majesty,
May pleasures on the day abound.
For I live in a land that's free,
And peace and justice can be found.

Beryl Mapperley

Her Majesty The Queen - April 2006

Her Majesty, our gracious Queen,
Has reached another milestone in her life.
Her service to the nation and her travels round the world
Have continued unabated over many decades.
Our Queen now, for over fifty years,
She's given a kindly welcome to the visitor
And spoken of her devotion to her task
And of her many interests in life.
As Head of State and of the Church
Her faithful service has given a rich consistent example to us all -
Stability and dignity, clarity of purpose,
And respect for all her subjects, young and old, rich and poor.

It is a joy to salute her on her eightieth birthday
And with loyal greetings wish her well.
We pray that God will bless her and her family
And keep them always in His care.
The nation should be humbly grateful
For the long eventful years that she has been among us.

Gwilym Beechey

Our Steadfast Rock

Does this country realise, I wonder
How fortunate we are
To possess our present monarch?
Parents, a hard act to follow
Yet she managed it delicately
With children a modern headache
She has never put a foot wrong
Impeccable behaviour always
Whether at home or abroad
Eighty years is a long time, Ma'am
To carry the burden of State
Long may your reign continue
You have kept this country great

B Williams

The Queen's 80th Birthday

Magnificent regal splendour
The Queen - our noble defender
Dripping epithets of glory
Tells a full life - and a colourful story
From the trials of war
To rationing no more
She has seen
A multi-ethnic Britain fit for a queen
A land at peace with itself and past
With the flag of destiny no longer at half mast
A foot soldier to tradition
She is capable of eloquent rendition
Of all that is pomp on our cherished soil
With the defeat of the enemy does our history embroil
The Buckingham Palace gates
Are there for he who waits
To see the changing of the guard
And bid the Queen on her eightieth kind regards.

Finnan Boyle

A Toast

With a majestic regal deportment,
Your people regard you as heaven-sent.
To figurehead of power, glasses raise,
For your eightieth birthday, we, you praise.

Often I wish I too had been crowned a queen,
Visiting all of the lands that you've seen.
To be waited on daily, hand and foot,
Not knowing feeling being covered in soot.

I don't have stamina to be royal,
Of your supreme status, remain loyal.
But you've grown into your occupation,
Ruling with style which befits our nation.

S Mullinger

An Easter Message - A Birthday Wish

Primroses and violets
Cuckoo and thrush's song
Catkins on the willow tree
Water lilies fringe the river bank
Stately like soldiers they stand

April with the call of spring
Pigeons on the wing
Rooks call from rickety nests
Squabbling over their ancient habitat

April with hills of green
Far away in faith, I see three crosses
On a sun-splashed horizon
Another anniversary, another Good Friday
Remembering Christ the Holy King of Kings
Crucified to redeem mankind

Remembering our gracious Queen
A special birthday wish I'm sending
Wishing you health and happiness
Strength to continue your reign over us
A royal challenge to sit on the throne
With God's grace you are not alone
Happy birthday our beloved
Queen Elizabeth

Frances Gibson

Faeries And Queens

Those who got near you
with bodies pressed on bollards
in streets lined with streamers
and droppings from high-up horses on guard
told me afterwards that your skin
was translucent and pale.
I imagined you were born of proud Titania
royal faerie queen of flutter and light touch
robed in gossamer, winged on fairy flight.
She gestured her hands over moss banks
and sipped from acorn cups.
You, Majesty, wave from battlements
and gold-adorned carriages.
You lift you lily-white gloved arm to
peering folk
who stretch to glimpse you through windows
in automobiles
flanked by security guards who tell me
that your handshakes remind them of feathers
which gracefully touch what's rough.
We, the common people, gaze at you
as we do a star on screen.
We log the memory in our archives to tell
others afterwards
'This is how it was'.

Gillian Muir

Easter 365

Each day can be like Easter
as daylight gives life to
our environment
after our grey bruised town
lies in state as night falls
in deep ultramarine.
So too air is breathed from
the lungs of the North Sea
causing the hairs on my arms
to stand erect as if paying
due respect to our Queen
as she celebrates another landmark birthday.
When I am brought back
to life out of my temporary
death called sleep
I go looking for you
like a dog tracking
the scent of its departed
master in the subtleties of
everyday life.

Laurence D E Calvert

Your Royal Majesty

Devoted daughter, sister, wife and a loving mother.
Raised to a position unlike any other.
Though you didn't choose this life, to us you've been most loyal.
These many years you've reigned as Queen, most elegant and royal.
When you acceded to the throne you pledged your dedication
To serve us well. Now may we join your birthday celebration?
Long live your gracious Majesty, this treasured precious life.
Devoted mother, grandmother, Queen and loving wife.

Margaret Doherty

Regal Steps

Dainty daffodil steps
propelled by Thor's thunder,
regal steps that know no fear,
snow-speckled gloves
like a peace sign of doves.
She signs treaties with a smile
that warms hearts like the River Nile.
Dainty smiles to make any foe
a friend, and a heart to
embrace the world
from head to toe.
A crown of fine silver
testifies of ancient wisdom
mirrored in the genteel gaze.

Hale Tsehlana

A Poem For Her Majesty

'Happy birthday, Ma'am
You're eighty today!'

The whole country will shout,
'Hip hip hooray'

You've eighty years under your belt
The nation's heart you shall melt

Everyone cheers and wishes you well,
'Hail Queen Elizabeth' we all shall yell

And there's one more thing I'd like to say
You are looking fantastic in every way.

Melissa Tindall (9)

The Birthday Girl - April 2006

'God Save The Queen'
Yes! I've sung that many a time.
'Tis a fine rousing song
With a good solid rhyme.
It makes me feel all proud
To have witnessed the great reign
Of a dear gracious lady
Queen Elizabeth by name.
May she grace the throne of England
To the joy of that great land
For many more faithful years
Just as the good Lord planned.
May she hear that anthem soaring
May she greet her subjects true
All waiting to gladly see
Her sovereignty shine through.
And may those eighty candles
Upon her birthday cake
Shine bright to light future ways
Her royal footsteps take.

Violet M Corlett

How Shall I Call You?

How shall I call you?
Most Gracious Lady? Your Royal Majesty?
Honoured and Respected Queen?
You are all of those and I salute you
On this auspicious year.
As a young woman you took up the task
With courage, dedication and determination
And have never faltered or failed.
Hard-pressed at times, on occasions sad,
But always delighting us with that wonderful smile.
God bless and keep you in all your waking days.
And should you dream at night
Dream of your loyal subjects
Raising their voices in heartfelt acclaim
To their beloved sovereign who has served them
                              through the years.
Hear them then as they give voice with pride,
God save our Lady Elizabeth,
God save the Queen!
God save the Queen.

Margaret Rose Harris

Eighty Today

Most gracious lady, may we honour you.
A celebration for all the things you do!
Now the list is endless, your duties are many.
You're always there, never missing any!
Happy-go-lucky, on your walkabout.
A gracious lady, without any doubt!
Preserving traditions and our way of life.
Perseverance through a lot of public strife!
You are a gem, a true national treasure.
Real caring, filling many hearts with pleasure!
Extending friendships, across foreign land.
Talking to the people, to better understand!
Unifying a nation, you raise their self-esteem.
Reigning successfully, you are a true queen!
Never has a monarch been so open and true.
So for this reason we, the people, admire you!
May your life be celebrated in style today.
An opportunity arises for the people to say
May you have the greatest birthday!

Annette Smith

Our Wonderful Queen

It would be nice to be seen
And sit with our Queen,
And to share her 80th birthday
She rules the land in every way
A very wonderful lady she is today,
And gives a smile when she meets
To stand must be hard on her feet,
Her colourful clothes are wonderful too
She knows a lot and knows what to do,
We wish her a very happy 80th birthday
It's Easter, we rejoice, as this is her day.

Joy Hall

The Queen's 80th Birthday

Incredibly, soon our queen eighty will be
Worthy a queen as any has been.
Her duties discharged admirably; thrilling her
Jubilee, when the country went on a spree
Proudest of nations, firework displays fired
The imagination, increasing our elation.

Enjoying African honeymoon at Treetops,
Came sad news, her father had died.
Naturally, our young queen cried.
Fortunately, she had firm support,
From Prince Philip, her handsome consort.
She rose to her challenge wonderfully,

As in World War Two did all the
Royal family, setting a fine example,
London Blitz presence superb sample
Of loyalty to their people.
With the little princesses doing their bit.
Never acting stuffy, our queen and sister

Margaret pitched-in, convinced by Churchill,
Like the populace, Britain, the war would win.
Came VE Day, the two girls from
'Buck House' slipped out joining
Anonymously, celebrating, empathy - creating.
Ascending the throne, has ruled splendidly,

Seeing prime ministers come and go,
Remaining undaunted, retaining her glow.
Supreme, every inch a queen, truly a dream
Marvelous to see her Golden Jubilee,
Long may she reign over you and me.

Graham Watkins

Paean

Hail to her Majesty, the Queen!
As noble a monarch as has ever been.
In time of war and in time of peace
Her devotion to duty does not cease.

Picture the child in the frothy dress,
And the girl in the uniform of the ATS,
Changing a wheel or checking the oil;
Vehicle maintenance for a royal.

Or the fairy-tale wedding in the Abbey Church -
To be followed so soon by a funeral march;
Her father's final battle with failing health,
And the years of war which advanced his death.
But . . .

When came the call to the royal throne,
She did not find herself alone
For standing steadfast at her side,
Stood he who won the royal bride,
(Himself of Grecian royal stock)
Became her anchor and her rock.

And now, at the age of fourscore years,
A grateful nation gives three cheers.
Long may Elizabeth o'er us reign!
But will England e'er see her like again?

John Coombes

A Birthday Gift To The Queen
(The Queen of England)

This is my birthday gift; this soothing verse
Written in rhyming couplets and made terse;

May you live long; oh 'Elizabeth the Queen'
And may your looks and strength be evergreen.

May your fame travel beyond Great Britain
Let it be known to all; you're now an octogenarian;

May your life be blissful oh Queen Betty,
As your name now rhymes with your age 'eighty'.

May your days on Earth be bright as the sun;
And be beautiful as its trail, when it's gone.

May the glittering stars be the sheen
That shine on your royal raiment, oh my Queen.

May your crown be filled with wisdom and power
And may your court be conducive as a garden bower.

May the moon stand in the centre
Of the heavens and empower your sceptre.

May your days be merry, this Easter season
For behind every merriment, there's a reason.

May your kingdom know no iniquity
And may you rule your people in amity.

May your birthday be historic;
And may you, to senility, be stoic.

Raymond A Uyok

Quintessentially . . .

Quintessentially
Unique
English
Extolled
Notable.

Happiness
Always
Pleasure
Personified.
Your day.

Be always
Inquiring
Righteous
Thorough
Happy
Devoted
Always
Yourself.

Helen Smith

Your Majesty

Oh Lilibet, your papa would have been proud
He may not have said it right out loud
But your unstinted devotion to the realm
Your unrelenting steadfastness at the helm

With the suddenness of responsibility
You may have doubted your own ability
But any insecurities have never shown
You have made this task your own

As a nation we salute you
As your subjects, we applaud you
For your dignity and fortitude
There is unending gratitude

Averil Fairey

My Royal Nightmare

It was an advert in the paper and it stated quite clear,
Poems wanted for our Queen who is eighty this year,
I wrote a poem and sent it to the address I had seen
Hoping it would be suitable for Her Majesty the Queen.

The Queen read my poem and thought it just right,
Then said to Prince Philip, 'This poet I must knight.'
I was called to the palace, most beautiful to see,
Then up to the Queen and got down on your knee.

The Queen, she just smiled, and I shuddered with fear,
The sword came down hard and cut off my right ear,
Then I awoke, my ear, it was on, I didn't have a pain,
Please don't let me have that bad nightmare again,

And if I ever get knighted let me make it quite clear,
Please be ever so careful and mind my right ear.

Thomas Dickinson

80th Birthday, Cake Of Memories

Cut the cake into eight slices,
Each slice representing ten years.
Look at each slice and remember
What you were doing, where you were.
Happy times, days filled with sunshine.
Sad memories? Wipe away tears.
Certain places, people, stand out.
Remember them all with fondness.
We cannot put the clock hands back
And time plays tricks with everyone,
Years ago seem like yesterday.
A lifetime spent serving country,
A true monarch, cherished by all,
May you enjoy many more years.

Angela Pritchard

The Queen
(On her birthday)

From horses, dogs, to army trucks, the Queen has done it all.
Her people really loved her, no one ever wanted her monarchy to fall.

The standards that she set,
Have never quite been equalled yet.

Her life has not been easy, she has had her share of woes,
But, she is always welcomed by the people where she goes.

I remember when the golden coach shone in the sun,
And my propelling pencil given to me at my school was then such fun.

The proud girl on a horse riding with her troops along The Mall,
On television some just black and white, but still she did not pall.

She will be remembered at the end of all our days,
Because she did her best for people quite set in their ways.

Jean Paisley

Queen Elizabeth II - 80th Birthday Verses

Your Majesty, Your Majesty
We wish you birthday joy
On this your special day -
And we pray that you continue
In good health along your way.

Your Majesty, Your Majesty
We thank you for who you are
Just a very special 'You' -
Always steadfast and reliable
In every single thing you do.

Your Majesty, Your Majesty
May you have many years ahead
To bless us with your grace -
Ruling over us with wisdom
And your dear familiar face.

A blessed and happy 80th birthday
To you - our 'Queen Elizabeth'.

Patricia Mary Saunders

Blessings On D-Day

Blessings on D-Day
For the world today
These celebrations
Involve all nations

It's been sixty years
Remembrance with tears
Many men were lost
Liberty's high cost

Sitting together
In sunny weather
The brave and the bold
On a beach called Gold

Mourning all who died
Hailing those survived
Hearing stories told
By war vets now old

Waiting patiently
For Her Majesty
Our lovely Queen
Cheering as she's seen

Memories invade
The soldiers parade
Sweetly bagpipes play
Bowing heads we pray

Speeches of respect
All without neglect
Times no one forgets
Medals pinned to vets

A royal tribute
Heroes we salute
Sadly it's the last
Past becoming past.

Ladee Basset

Elizabeth Our Queen

In nineteen hundred and twenty-six,
A little girl was born.
To Elizabeth and George,
On an April morn.

With her sister and the corgis,
She had time for play.
Never ever realising,
She would be Queen one day.

A mechanic in the army,
Doing her bit for the war.
Seeing the bombs fall on London,
With the enemy at the door.

Being taken to South Africa,
When she met the man of her dreams,
But destiny always finds a way,
To bring happiness it seems.

Becoming a wife and a mother
Loving her children day by day,
But troubles were there to beset her,
As troubles sometimes may.

But now is her eightieth birthday,
With strength she has come sailing through,
From one loyal subject and husband,
Birthday greetings, Ma'am, are wished for you.

Peggy Howe

With Thanks To The Queen

Eighty years of her wonder
Many years of her reign
Eighty years her country
Has always stood to gain.

Caring, loving and kind
Are the things that cross my mind
As to the best qualities there can be
And in the Queen, these I can see.

She shows admiration and care
For her family, she'll always be there
But for her people she will be as well,
For eighty years she has to tell.

Her birthday is something we should celebrate
But not big enough is one small fete
So we should all unite together
And be thankful for what she has done, forever.

The lives of the people she has made better
I know for one that they will never forget her
She is a role model for the young and old
For she is courageous, strong and bold.

On behalf of the country I would like to say
Thank you, to the Queen on her throne today
And with our respect, we must pay,
Long to reign, let's hope she may

Kerrie Washington

The Queen's 80th Birthday

To be in charge of the royal scene
quite a tough task for the Queen
she has to put up with a lot of strain
during the period of her reign

By now she reaches 80 years of age
observing the world from her golden cage
she may look back with a twinkle in her eye
yet still be linked with a heavy sigh

All the people of the British Isles
have followed her with amicable smiles
since the very day of her birth
along her path on this Earth

Since World War Two they bestowed on her praise
they loved their Queen, her charm, her grace
they never stop to wish her well
along with the tinkle of Big Ben's bell
cheering her and the royal scene
blessed be England and long live the Queen.

Wila Yagel

Queen's 80th

What a great lady we've come to know
Warmth and comfort she does show
Who sometimes wears a crown upon her head
I guess she takes it off when she goes to bed.

She looks quite splendid on her walks
Quite often to her people she talks
Who looks very regal, walks with a good pace
Who greets her people with a smiling face.

So, Ma'am, on your 80th birthday
With much love, we all would like to say
Good health and long life for many a year
Full of happiness, and not many a tear.

M Shaw

EIIR - At 80 2006

How lucky we've been
With you as our Queen:
Gracious, noble and true,
Who could not admire you?
To duty devoted,
Dedication well noted;
By your faith sustained,
Our reverence you've gained.
Steadfast and concerned,
Nothing has your head turned:
Grave yet good humoured,
Oft amused, it is rumoured.
Clever, wise and witty,
Always ready with pity.
A cherishing wife
Steeped in family life,
Loving our country
And all the Earth's bounty.
Long may you yet reign
And live years, without pain.

N D Wood

A Poem For The Queen

Greetings sincere to our wonderful Queen
Who beside the good times many troubles has seen.
But to the public a brave face she shows
What she is feeling nobody knows.
Now she is eighty she still looks serene
A wife, mother, grandmother and queen.
Her Majesty is always on call
A shining example to one and all
With good health and happiness long may she reign
I, an admiring loyal subject, remain.

Joyce Strong

Long Live The Queen!

Long live the Queen!
Long live the Queen!
Seldom heard, seldom seen
She takes life at a canter
Oh, how I wish that I could meet her
So we could have a little banter.

Oh how great it would be
To take one's cup of tea
With our Queen, Her Majesty
Defender of our Faith, our laws
And though she is our sovereign
She's been caught out doing chores.

For decades she has been
Our hope, our inspiration, our Queen
Head of State, yet humble in her rule
A hero who is dignified
And in my eyes that's cool.

Her dignity, authority and power
Is given from God above
In order to serve her subjects
To share His peace and love.

Our subordinate Queen
To the King of Kings above
Rules her land, with peace and love
That she holds in trust, for God above.

Now eighty, and still she carries on
Still graciously uplifts us, inspires us to be strong
When evil in our nation, seems to gain control
Our monarch serves a vital role
As a Christian monarch should
To inspire us in our faith
And overcome bad with good.

She reminds us to be strong
When all around is fear
So the Queen, our Christian monarch
I will hold quite dear and say
Long live the Queen!

Mark Walker

Happy Birthday, Ma'am

We went up to London
To see the Queen,
To a garden party,
The first time we'd been.

I saw Harold Wilson,
He smiled at me
Near a large marquee
Where we queued for tea.

His wife was wearing
A flimsy dress.
How clever, I thought,
She's a poetess.

I've still got my dress
And the shoes and the hat
But where is the bag?
One's been looking for that!

The invitation came
All printed in gold,
Almost forty years ago,
And now we are old.

Rachel E Joyce

For Her Majesty's 80th Birthday

Happy birthday, Your Majesty.
Congratulations and good health.
You have triumphed in adversity.
Stood firm in good times and in death.
My memories stretch way behind
To a childhood in far-distant Nepal,
Where my father whispered 'Everest climbed
But keep it a secret until tomorrow.'
My youthful heart swelled with pride
To keep such a mystery to myself.
I could not watch your carriage ride
But imagined the pomp and circumstance.
Since then I've been a constant fan
And proud to live in this great land.

Meg Atkins

Glorious Majesty

Glorious, wonderful Majesty,
Highly esteemed Queen of the nation,
Shining paradigm of royalty,
Admired without reservation.

Glorious, wonderful Majesty,
A smile, and a twinkle in your eyes,
Showing the best of the monarchy,
Truly commanding, regal and wise.

Glorious, wonderful Majesty,
A queen, wife, mother, and grandmother,
Respected for your fine modesty,
Strength of a woman like no other.

Glorious, wonderful Majesty,
To do your best is your endeavour,
Always trusted for your honesty,
God save you and bless you forever.

Gillian Jones

Hail The Queen

Hail! The Queen of United Kingdom
And its territories!
With graciousness,
She attends her duties
With a
Serene smile and a hand wave

Always wonderful
To see her and her family
On the balcony
After any event

To be born is something
To celebrate one's 80th birthday
Is a dream
Fulfilled

Many, many happy returns
May she reign
For many more years
To come.

Efua Sam-Avor

A Poem For Her Majesty

If only I could meet you,
To wish you happiness and cheer,
On this very special birthday,
For each and every year,
Although I've never met you,
You're always in my heart,
Happy birthday Ma'am,
Our sovereign,
Queen of Hearts.

Rachael Milsted

Great Britain

Her Majesty the Queen rides along on a great thoroughbred horse
Her Majesty often astride this great but unwieldy creature
Does show it how; richer or poorer; for better or worse
It should perform its duty; wear its shiny shoes in the global arena

At times it seems to raise its hooves up really much too far
Still the Queen carries on her positive example regardless
When Her Majesty dismounts and goes to Balmoral by car
The trusty steed gallops on itself, hard-working and relentless

When frequently the horse becomes more difficult
Flares and scoffs its great nostrils at its past not future
The Queen clicks her heels and trots it round and about
Pats it and shows it the rich activity of our nation's culture

By giving the example of her sovereignty and duty
The Queen highlights beauty; enhances Commonwealth and nation
Holding in her royal hands the regal reins of monarchy
Exceeds her duty; Great Britain gives her a standing ovation!

Thank you Your Majesty.

Sheila Cheesman

Happy And Glorious

Eighty years have sped by fast
We have noticed changes in the past,
Some have been good but some didn't last
But for our noble Queen the die was cast.

So we say well done, Your Majesty, we offer you best wishes
You have seen our country rise from the ashes.
Those war years saw our lives take unlimited bashes
In wartime the country suffered from many gashes.

Pondering in our hearts what might have been
A most fortunate people to have you on the scene,
The grass on our side of the fence is incredibly green
So we all raise a cheer and say, 'God bless the Queen.'

John V Waby

The Queen

Her Royal Highness, long may she reign
Her honesty and steadfastness brought her fame
In Commonwealth affairs she was a sight to behold
A bastion of strength, so we have been told
Through her own bereavements leaving much sorrow
She regained her composure and acted normal on the morrow
The Queen, so regal in her grief, so it appears
Encounters multitudes of admirers, listen to the cheers
Her fondness of animals, she contrived a *dorgi*
A dachshund dog crossed with a Welsh corgi
Elizabeth Alexandra Mary Windsor as she was baptised
Imparts a feeling of pride, you can tell by her eyes
She gives one a feeling of being of true British descent
Let's hope the Queen lives out her life, happy and content.

Francis Arthur Rawlinson

Your Majesty

I can't remember Britain
when you were not the Queen,

whatever else has happened
you have always been
the constant in a changing world,
the jewel in England's crown
while politicians wax and wane,
while scams and scandals swirl around
you stand, example to us all,
a slave to princely duty,
obedient to your country's call
and clothed in regal beauty,

a living, loving symbol
of what Britain ought to be,
an ageing lady, like my mum;
my Queen, you'll do for me.

Valerie Sutton

Our Gracious Queen

Many lovely ladies have graced the worldwide scene,
yet none with more fulfilment than our loyal, splendid Queen.
Elizabeth they called her, or Lilibet for short,
the gift of God in wisdom to the nations brought.

Her happy smile belies the burden of a crown,
which, through all events, has never let her down.
Perhaps idyllic childhood gave our future Queen
a cheerful, loving purpose and a faith serene.

The two princesses playing around their royal home
in their cottage, with their corgis, free to roam -
had time for other children, to televise their care
and sympathy in wartime - the world each had to bear.

Great jubilation present on war cessation day.
Flags and celebrations came the royal way.
Empire countries gladly joined our central family
as thousands watched them wave and smile on their balcony.

Soon Elizabeth and Philip made the perfect pair.
No one could have found a finer man to share
in family and royalty as husband to our Queen.
Strong in taking over where King George had been.

Queen Elizabeth, we love your ways, your kindness and your grace.
Your tireless charm, the warmth of fun always in your face.
We hope your reign continues on for many a decade yet,
your early promise to your people, few of us forget.

A Audrey Agnew

God Bless You Ma'am

God bless you Ma'am
Your humble servant I am
You've looked after our nation,
Made duty your destination,
A Taurean by birth
You've proved your worth,
A Christian woman,
A dutiful wife,
You've seen Britain through years of strife,
Apollo 8 and the space console,
World War II to the advent of rock 'n' roll,
Looking back through the years
Many smiles and a few tears,
How proud am I to be of this realm,
With you at the helm
You've steered your ship through many dangers,
Always have a smile for strangers,
Though you may be weary,
You've always kept bright and cheery.
So for all the many changes in life,
Though there have been wars,
Your army bore the brunt of scars
Britannia's fortune is in the stars
This is why I wish you a special wish today
Three cheers for Queen Elizabeth, hip hip hooray!

Alan Pow

Let All The Nation Sing

Let all the hills rejoice,
Let all the mountains sing,
Oh! what joy to the nation's hearts
of oak this happy day brings;
Let forty guns bark their salute
across this land,
Let the billows roll in rhythmic beat
over coastal sands.

Let all the feathered dawn chorus
together sing,
Let all the church bells joyously ring,
God bless Her Majesty in this, her
triumphant 80th year,
Our first lady of these sceptred isles
we hold so very dear.

So let's all fill our glasses and partake
of a loyal toast on this happy scene,
As we wish a happy and wonderful
birthday to Her Majesty The Queen!

Peter Morriss

Lost Moment

I think it was Jubilee year, if my memory serves me right,
When you honoured Ripley with a visit, the locals to delight.
With sun shining brightly, and bunting made,
Everyone excited when they saw the cavalcade.
Alas! Not so, for one small boy
In Cub Scout uniform, Mother's pride and joy.
You selected him to speak to,
Didn't know what to do,
Suddenly struck dumb,
Sorry Mum!
Normally you couldn't shut him up,
The boy next to him couldn't believe his luck.
As he answered for him with a grateful look,
God bless you, Ma'am, for him you chose,
Maybe it was his angelic pose.
Memories flood, the time it does fly.
Now you are eighty! Twinkle still in your eye.
He's no longer a boy, he's grown up too,
But you can bet he's still teased for not talking to you.

Rosemary Cresswell

A Shared Experience

Congratulations and celebrations came for Elizabeth our Queen,
Always smiling, very caring, with a smart hat seen.
On 21st April, year 2006, a remarkable 80 years was she,
With fifty-four years dedication as Queen given constantly.
Ninety-nine ladies had surprise invites at the palace for tea,
As they all shared this same special birthday you see!

Prince Charles arranged a dinner for the royal family to celebrate
A wonderful family gathering for a wonderful mother who was great.
After morning church, when walking outside, the local people she met,
Children curtsied, gave her flowers, a day they will never forget!
The TV cameras and newsmen followed the Queen everywhere,
The whole world was watching her, always smiling, showing
                                                 interest and care.

Not to be forgotten, it was also England's famous St George's Day,
His flag was flying, many double celebrations were on the way.
In Birmingham, in honour of Her Majesty's birthday was
                                                 'Beating the Retreat',
Bands played, Morris men danced and St George and the Dragon
                                        puppet show was a family treat.
A truly shared experience everywhere, you really must agree,
I wish Her Majesty good health, peace and longevity.

Stella Bush-Payne

Conqueror Of Hearts

Though born in a dynasty of great conquerors,
Founded by William the Great Conqueror,
Queen Elizabeth's never been a conqueror of
Territories as Her Majesty's,
Always wanted to be a conqueror of hearts like
A spectacular performer of arts.

The petals of love and affection,
That Her Majesty's been receiving throughout her reign,
From the people of Britain and her colonies spontaneously,
Speak volumes on her skills to conquer hearts.

By disposition and temperament,
Her Majesty's been like a loving and caring mother,
To all the people of Britain and her colonies,
Irrespective of their castes, colours, creeds or sexes.

Her Majesty's practices of congratulating centenarians,
And couples celebrating their diamond wedding anniversaries,
Of UK and Commonwealth over the years stand as standing
Testimonies to her tastes of chaste to laud great achievers.

In the changing role of a monarch from the actual power-wielder,
To the virtual powerless titular head, Her Majesty's set an example,
As to how a nominal head's to function,
Without any records of discords, admirably and enviously.

Davis Akkara

God Bless The Queen

God bless the Queen of England
Clothed with honour and majesty
God bless the United Kingdom
Made out ultimately like the Heaven's curtains
God bless the people of England
The waters that stood above the mountains
God bless the united nations that comes out of her
That they get their meat in due seasons
God bless the root of Her Majesty
That they continually dwell in prosperity
Uprightly given to generations unborn
God bless the works of the Queen
That nations in captivity be set free
God bless those who daily praise the Queen
That they among many be enveloped in Her Majesty
God bless me
That my name be written on the golden plaque
Of the book of Edinburgh
God bless the Queen forever.

Oludotun Fajorin

Happy Birthday Your Highness

Our grand old mum
Long may she live
No greater do they come
Such stature she gives

Eight decades of grace
Eight decades, mum of the people
Upholds the Queen Mother's place
Always so very regal

We wish you long life
Our love and respect, forever keen
Through good times and strife
We pray, 'Long live our Queen!'

Happy birthday, Your Highness
Long may you reign
England without Your Highness
Just wouldn't be the same.

Ferrell L 'Huck' Hickson

My Memories From 1956 To 2006

I first saw Her Majesty
When I looked at my father in uniform
He an officer and I a child in oblivion
Gazing in awe and wonder at the metallic coin
Shining with colour, grandeur and royalty;
Oh Father! What's that you are wearing?
This is the King and this is Queen Elizabeth
HRH The Queen of England -
Neither Queen nor England did I know then
I smiled, I was happy and I felt good,
So gracefully smart in his army service dress my father stood.
The second time I saw Your Majesty, was real!
As a schoolgirl, in my city, a rare chance,
When all of a sudden the motorcade came and I
Standing on the road, got a passing glance -
The royal visit to Pakistan in 1961 -
Your Majesty I saw you and treasured the view;
Your Majesty, we have always wished well and prayed for you;
Your country is loved, your people inspire
We share your history and grand attire;
And I am especially proud to be,
A member of a family honoured by thee;
So I take this lifetime opportunity
To wish you a most precious special 'Happy Birthday' -
Wrapped and ribboned with
A gift of words, of respect, affection and prayer
May Your Majesty live long and be forever the light of liberty!
I, a born refugee, never saw the land where I was born
I wonder now - is it freedom enchained or freedom attained?
Would my wish be ever fulfilled, to make a home in your land?
And to treasure the jewel of seeing you again?
May you have many many more happier returns of the day
Once again, Your Majesty, please accept a very, very Happy Birthday.

Anjum Wasim Dar

The Queen (Public And Private)

Subject: Elizabeth, Queen, calm and serene
With your hair so tidily curled,
'Neath a hat with a feather
In inclement weather
You step out and enter our world.

Queen: Dear subject, that is one's public face.
One has to be well turned out.
One can't face the press
In a shabby old dress
But it would be comfy no doubt.

Subject: Elizabeth, Queen, we revere and esteem,
Admire all the work that you do.
Those far, foreign places
And millions of faces
And all of them looking at you.

Queen: Dear subject, your praise is too lavish.
One is blessed with a stiff upper lip.
But I admit exhibitions
And all politicians
Honestly give one the pip!

Subject: Elizabeth, Queen, are you all that you seem?
So gracious, so tireless, so neat.
Do you long to flop down,
And fling off your crown,
And watch Coronation Street?

Queen: Dear subject, your comments are noted
And yes, I would love to be *me!*
But the gold chains that bind
Are there to remind
That a Queen can never be free.

Georgina Percivall

Happy Birthday

H appy birthday to the Queen
A day of joy especially for you
P resents to unwrap
P resents to make you smile
Y our smiles will last all day.

B irthdays are always great
I hope you enjoy it
R eady to party
T onight is party night
H aving fun is what it's about
D oing what you want to do
A nd do what you do only once a year
Y ou should enjoy it while it lasts.

' T is also Easter
O verjoyed kids waiting for the day.

T he excitement builds up
H appy children endure their eggs
E ach one making them happy.

Q ueuing up for the eggs
U have to please kids
E aster eggs make everyone happy
E ven the adults
' N ever too old,' they say.

Louise Smith

Happy Birthday

At 25 years old, Queen Elizabeth II, crowned
Mother of four children
Gruelling long tours abroad with her consort
Met many prime ministers

Great scientific, medical, railway revolutions
Airways, Concorde, television, digital, computers
Pioneering, films, great stars era 'Gone With The Wind'
Problems, asylum seekers, integration, cultural

Causing worldwide difficulties
Irish, American, bombings, Earl Mountbatten killed
Buckingham Palace internally managerial streamlined
Fashions change, throwaway age

Princess Diana's tragic death
Her children, divorce, gay civil contracts introduced
Death of the beloved Queen Mother
Queen's love of horse racing

Charles and Camilla, international duties with dedication
Queen now 80 years, having wealth of experience, invaluable
The great support of her consort, Prince Philip
Her devotion to serve, carve her name with pride.

Patricia Turpin

The Queen's 80th Birthday

Special are these years to the Queen, every event she has seen.
She was quite young when she went to the throne, now her life won't
be her own.
'Old head on young shoulders' it changed her life, then from being a
teenager she became a wife.
The blessing of children came her way, it brought such joy,
she would say.
Always on show, she would have to be, cameras clicking for
papers or TV.
Every occasion the Queen attends, in luxury and splendour
she has to spend.
Lots of trouble and strife she's seen, through her lifetime
special people have been.
The birth of grandchildren brought so much joy, toasting their lives,
some girls some boys.
Family photos they stand and pose, in Buckingham Palace
the family grows.
The Queen loves her horses and loves to ride, all around the
countryside, also her beloved corgis and her Labrador too,
the Queen loves them all, they love her too.
Prince Charles likes to visit, they take a walk, round the garden
they have a good talk. They catch up on things that mother and son
do, Prince Charles talks to flowers, they're a beautiful view.
Around the world she has been, doing her duty as a queen.
The Queen's been around for eighty years, there's been some
laughter and some tears.
But she's been strong through and through, there'll be no other
to compare to you.
She takes a walk round the crowds, she loves her public,
they shout out loud.
Beautiful and radiant on this special day, everyone shouts
hip hip hooray.
There's lots of presents, flowers too, she gathers them up and
says, 'Thank you.'
She'll have a sleep and a rest, so at night she'll be her best.
All the family meet this day, they're so proud you'll hear them say.
Queen Elizabeth is there to reign, on the throne she shall remain.

Sandra Bentley

Your Majesty!

From one of your subjects, and family our wishes true
The hopes that you enjoy your birthday, all you do!
That the years ahead allow you good health, joy
As we know you will still hold the faith diligence employ
In all you do, with a smile, though, some joy!
Like my wife and I, just a little older than you now
Have had advantage of seeing our family grow to adults!
Still with pride of county, country Queen we vow!
This England would be a very different place without your touch!
That inspires, by word, also deed, so very much
As you serve us, so we shall serve you in dignity, touch!
Consider us as a part of your huge family, as we are
Who even as a mother you stand by our sides evils to bar!
I am a veteran, also a survivor, as you are as well!
Know that time holds rewards, and that when stories you tell
Will show the glory and courage always given with heart,
Despite the heavy burdens carried as Princess , Queen from early start
On this 80th anniversary I'm sure the world will loudly voice
God save the Queen, mean it with love, their choice.

There are things we don't forget! For me, being in a Guard of Honour
When you attended a school or college near Bath.
It had rained heavy before your arrival, we were polished up
But quite wet! You got out of your transport, changing your shoes,
Then queen-like walked along our ranks! Provided by the 4th Btn, The Somerset LI (PA) TA.

Happy birthday! May there be many more!

Edgar E Poole

A Tribute To Her Majesty

A salute to Her Majesty
For all that she has been;
From the day that she was crowned
And became our beloved Queen.
For all her many attributes
On view for all to see;
When carrying out her duties
Which she takes so responsibly.
Her smile and her little wave
To the crowds as she rides by;
The moments when she'll stop and chat
Or maybe dry her eye.
Moments of sadness, moments of joy,
Especially when Charles was born,
Her first little boy!
For her duties they are many
In this land and overseas;
It must be very difficult,
Everyone to please.
But she carries on unthwarted,
Determined to fulfil;
What can only be described,
As her calling and God's will.

Peter R Beadle

Our Queen

When I was a little lass my mother said to me
'Your father's ordered a surprise, just you wait and see'
The telly came in black and white, I hadn't seen one before
I was filled with great delight and watched you in awe

A princess in a golden coach filled our television screen
Tears of happiness ran down my face, as you became our Queen
All through my life you've been there and then my dream came true
For you came and opened Sullom Voe and I stood next to you

I would've loved to hug you as if you were my friend
As through the cheering happy crowd on your way you did wend
Your lovely smile and twinkling eyes sometimes hide a veil of tears
I saw you suffer bravely throughout your 80 years

So, Ma'am, you have inspired me as you went on your way
My four oldest children won a prize on your Silver Jubilee day
I'll never forget how hard you work, you make us very proud
If you were in ragged clothes you'd stand out in a crowd

With kindly nod and wave of hand, loyal, royal
Through and through
I'd like to say God bless you and a happy birthday too.

Natalie Opray

The Crown

Mornings evolve in speed . . .
like a fast wind, words follow
one another,
emotions scrambled in seconds . . . touches turn into the rush . . .
instead of peace . . .
endless mazes of history,
of pain, sorrow, pride . . .
endless confusion
in the colours of the crown.
. . .
history runs . . . Queen glorifies the day
history screams, but the lady's eyes remain
. . .
love
clams things down.
Fingers regain their shape,
the head . . .
being able to think . . . suddenly talks
about the crown . . . the ages of
delight
receive the message . . .
the Queen
the life
the crown
make sense.

Jasmina Trifunovic

Our Majesty The Queen

Nineteen-twenty-six the year
Twenty-first of April the date,
The birth of our dear monarch
When Elizabeth first met her fate.

A devoted sovereign throughout her realm
Travelling the wide world over,
She does her duty without complaint
For her it is truly no bother.

Your life complete with family four
And grandchildren there are seven,
Much pleasure into your life have brought
Indeed must be like Heaven.

Blessed with Philip your loving spouse
From old age you have no fear.
You always look so young and fit
Look forward to a joyful year.

Now many years have come and gone
All taken in your stride.
When looking back with happy thoughts
Survey your life with pride.

We thank you, Ma'am, from all our hearts
And a long reign amidst us will stay,
God bless you on your eighty years
As birthday greetings we send your way.

Rosalind Sim

Congratulations

The Queen at eighty,
Glorious in old age,
Still true to duty,
Turns another page;
As bells ring out
'Mid cheers along the way,
And guns salute
To mark this happy day,
By many years of service
She has done,
Our hearts and loyalty
She has won;
So she continues,
Steadfast, on she goes,
With grace and charm,
Each year it grows;
Wife and mother,
All close to her heart,
The Duke still at her side,
He played his part;
Her many tours abroad
A huge success,
And countless duties here,
At home, no less;
And so, for all the years
Of dedication, we send you
Wishes true, in affirmation,
Happy birthday, Ma'am,
Long may you reign supreme,
Elizabeth, a truly noble Queen.

Dorothy Neil

Oh Great Queen

Your Majesty, the mother of nations
North and south are all your provinces
East and west are all your dominions
The Queen that rules from coast to coast

Her Majesty that commands
The respect of all her subjects
The ever refreshing Queen of England
The great one that dwells in the castle

Your Majesty, your reigns spread across the continents,
Your love for all is quite magnificent,
Because of the roles you've played in lives of many
You feed the poor and cover the homeless

Your kindness and mercy has saved a million
That might have died of hunger all around the world
Oh great Queen! I heard that you bear Elizabeth
That's the name of the mother of John the Baptist

Who was the forerunner of Jesus Christ that saves the world
May your reign bring more peace to the world
May your domination ever flourish to all the nations
Even as you turn eighty years old today

We shall never forget your splendour
Your magnificency shall ever remain with us
We shall never regret your living
Oh great Queen! You are the mother

Of many generations yet unborn
Long live the Queen of England
Long live the Mother of Nations
The elegant Queen that is full of passion.

Adegoke Austin Adedamola

Children Of The Empire

It was the year of the coronation, just before
The Empire started flocking to Britain, and
The Royal family was just a grey photo
Of white people in a newspaper, or
A sudden arrival in a far-flung country, when
The people flocked to stand along roads
Waving stiff, red, white and blue pennants,
To watch a swift cavalcade go by,
So quick you'd miss the pale face in the feather'd hat
Inside the big shining car. 1952 was different.
Children all over the world stood in lines,
Pulled from their classes onto a dusty, cold playground
In Southern Africa, or a vivid green clearing
Overhung with heavy clouds in the tropics
For a brief address by the head teacher. We heard
The news of a new Queen, a beautiful young Queen
In a silk gown embroidered with all the flowers of her Empire.
Flame lilies and proteas, orchids, roses and daffodils,
And we held out our hands, tawny, tanned and pale,
For a wonderfully heavy half-crown and a pencil
Wrapped in the colours of her Union Jack.

Liz Davies

A Royal In The Ribble

There's been a lot of rumour
That should the Queen retire.
Her Majesty has expressed a wish
To come to Lancashire.

To live in the Ribble Valley
Which nestles in the hills.
Steeped in the local history
Of coal mining and the mills.

To feel the witches' presence
See hand-crafted wooden clogs.
To stroll the paths of Pendle
With her darling corgi dogs.

We can't promise you a castle, Ma'am
Or a palatial grand retreat.
Just a pretty little cottage
In a pleasant cobbled street.

You'd find there's something special
For you - Your Majesty,
We'd make you very welcome
With a right royal cup o'tea.

Joyce Graham

For The Queen

A favourite mother,
the populace are
comfortable with
your effortless image.
At ease, never pushy,
your loyalty and
commitment constant.
On duty day or night,
you are steady, sober.
Pomp and ceremony
proffered to us through
your genuine gentility.

Always, your smiling
face, beneath the hat
sedate and neat, while
pearls give a glow
to your ageless skin.
Surrounded by servants
and your corgis, ever
available for scrutiny
by people who continue
to keep you in power.
Your energy and good
health, an inspiration.

It is no great wonder
why we all want to wish
you happy 80th birthday.

Mary Guckian

The Queen And I

We've been together all our lives, the Queen and I
Since the fun and cheer of the coronation year
With tins of sweets and special treats
Street parties everywhere in 1953
Red, white and blue on land and sea
We were young and carefree then, the Queen and I

God, King and country were our values then
Women struggled for equality with men
She won our hearts right from the start - our sovereign
As a young man I entered the nursing profession
And progressed to the top in steady procession
We broke new ground together, the Queen and I

Then came all the troubles of 1992
Oh! Your Majesty it was my annus horribilis too
Family break up or was it break down?
I saved my life you salvaged the crown
To those dreadful days we wave a dignified goodbye
We have suffered together, the Queen and I

Now after 53 years of excellent reign
The nation honours this noble octogenarian
Ma'am, you would restore my faith in the monarchy once again
If on your honour's list you would include my name
It needn't be a knighthood, an OBE would suffice for me!
But if yet again you should forget I still wish you happy birthday, Lilibet

Bill Campbell

God Bless Our Queen

Radiant and beautiful
A pleasure to see,
With workload impossible,
Yet duty's the key.
She has always been there
When the going was tough
And our country was threatened
And we'd all had enough.
As brave as her parents
When the bombs whistled down,
Her thought was for others
In her uniform brown,
She drove through the Blitz
Giving aid on her way,
Compassionate and cheerful,
Terror, fear to allay.
Her love for her people
Is boundless and pure,
A jewel of rare quality
Through her life to endure,
Give a toast to Her Majesty -
The Queen of us all,
Let's live by example
And follow her call!

Valma June Streatfield

Anchor Books Information

We hope you have enjoyed reading this book - and that you will continue to enjoy it in the coming years.

If you like reading and writing poetry drop us a line, or give us a call, and we'll send you a free information pack.

Alternatively if you would like to order further copies of this book or any of our other titles, then please give us a call or log onto our website at
www.forwardpress.co.uk

**Anchor Books Information
Remus House
Coltsfoot Drive
Peterborough
PE2 9JX**

(01733) 898102